Collected Sonnets

Also by Gavin Selerie:

Playground for the Working Line (Ziesing Brothers, 1981)
Azimuth (Binnacle Press, 1984)
Puzzle Canon (Spectacular Diseases, 1986)
Strip Signals (Galloping Dog Press, 1986)
Elizabethan Overhang (Spectacular Diseases, 1989)
Southam Street (New River Project, 1991)
Tilting Square (Binnacle Press, 1992)
Roxy (West House Books, 1996)
Danse Macabre, with Alan Halsey et al
(Ispress & West House Books, 1997)
Days of '49, with Alan Halsey (West House Books, 1999)
Vitagraph (Binnacle Press, 2001)
Le Fanu's Ghost (Five Seasons Press, 2006)
The Canting Academy, with David Annwn et al (Ispress, 2008)
Music's Duel. New and Selected Poems 1972–2008
(Shearsman Books, 2009)
Hariot Double (Five Seasons Press, 2016)

Gavin Selerie

Collected Sonnets

Shearsman Books

First published in the United Kingdom in 2019 by
Shearsman Books
50 Westons Hill Drive
Emersons Green
BRISTOL
BS16 7DF

Shearsman Books Ltd Registered Office
30–31 St. James Place, Mangotsfield, Bristol BS16 9JB
(this address not for correspondence)

www.shearsman.com

ISBN 978-1-84861-689-9

Cover image
Josef Albers
Variant of "Related," ca. 1940
Oil on Masonite
16 1/2 x 13 1/8 in. (41.9 x 33.3 cm)
The Josef and Anni Albers Foundation, 1976.1.1052

Photo: Tim Nighswander/Imaging4Art

Photo of the author: Barbara Große

CONTENTS

Early Poems / *Azimuth* and after 1969–1986

Elizabethan Overhang 1987–1988

Tilting Square 1988–1991

Deep Passes 1992

Twisted Circle 1994–1999

Danse Macabre (Recension) 1997

Days of '49 outtakes 1997–1999

Between Tongues 2007–2010

from *Hariot Double* 2009–2016

Motley 2010–2014

Land Spokes 1999–2019

Out of an English Pole 2017

Tuning Tomorrow 2018–2019

Early Poems
/
Azimuth and after

1969-1986

Physics

'Bloody' Roberts, we called him
in a desperate spell, cursing
as he matched our would-be Terror,
his iron skull and forearm
levered from a teak redoubt
ready to bawl or cuff
whoever dared, green or red,
block the scope of electron law.

What power and guilt arose in the gullet
when, trooping into chapel, we heard
how—crushed in a lorry's jack-knife
on the bend of a nearby hill—
our monster was dismantled
leaving nothing for us to know.

Blue Vent

Where we came in the dark with vague directions
an endless road uphill then a bumpy track
into the valley, with ghost chimneys and the sea
a muffled roar—to pitch a tent, make love and sleep
the seagulls screeching as broken tin

wondrous morning the water turquoise the hillside
strewn with heather—gorse flowers yellow
round a stream cutting through to boulders, rocks
and a patch of sand

campfire song, man and pebble speaking a secret
between gaunt cliffs—and then the rain at 6 am
a gale to shift guyropes and poles, a lashing
that even the trench won't defeat, we must crawl
drenched and numb till sun reverses the flood

Trevellas Porth, 1969

Translation

An oak armchair and red oriental rug, a candle
on the marble mantelpiece, a pile of books
by a closed door

the flame burns green then breaks into ruby specks—
I am something looking at myself, skull solid and smooth
as a peanut

its case opens and plunges up, a cloud silky white
that hovers over a vast plain

I hear the slow soft trail of her voice
that holds me inside, a bird a leaf a snake
in a glowing tract

each thing has its place filtered crystal or black
through the strands of our hair
as we let the go die and pass into other space

Lyric Folds

for Celia Humphris

A branch presses on the glass, it's a phrase
from an old ballad where a rose grows
out of a lover's brain and the singer asks
does she know the face she dreams

    a text carried to another shore
    comes back as the moon
    tinging a silk sheet

can't tell the meaning in reason, can't fathom
that blood in the stream

    a jewelled electric darts
    between curls acoustic, rigged
    over bass, cymbal and snare

angel harsh her voice lingers and soars
chest deep to touch the sky

River Map

Days melt into each other and it's always twilight
where the yarrow stalks are thrown
(I am the handle to be grasped I am spokes
burst out of the wheel)

                    she speaks piano and vibes
as the ceiling gauze turns purple
and a double-decker ladder
slides across the wall

lip to lip the bed floats—
a glossy record sleeve—fingers
in a pick-up head—the things' side
                    of it—are they letting us go

milk courses through you   a twisting tide
in the house beneath   writes its baffled outline

Wheeldale

Bilberry tufts
creeping ripe and black
beneath heather shade

burnt rainbow rippling
in an eastern breeze,
the curlew, a herdsman's harp

prickly furze a line of wake
to Raven stones
grooved over the gill

jaw to belly
with gurgle steps

Wade's causeway
a slab diagonal
leading won't say where

The Line

Hugged the bracken ridge to Lastingham
and bent down in St Mary's crypt
with the needle jigging

found interlaced serpents
and a hogback with a bear on guard

from this hollow squat I drank moments
of a thing on another laid

and went over Black Howe
and through the Bridestones
to Dargate Dikes in pine-raw solitude

saw them from there and couldn't
get away—globes or radomes
glistening on black plinths
in a far vigilanus whose secrets may leak

Sheriff Hutton Castle

The craggy giant holds up one arm
brown sandstone from the hills around,
a northern thickness on the first moor-ledge
made gaunt from warring and intrigue

naked ground in the forest of Galtres
that you plunge down on from the upper road
or swing in on from the lower glassy curve,
proud lines dispersed as lonely prisoners
the court a farmyard with pigs and a haystack

here destinies were dreamed and fleshed
in a garland with flourishes and blots—
above the moat bagpipes droned a dance
tawny satin clung to bedposts
while harts and hinds stirred in the mist

Rude Stone

I am come I know not how   as seawood tossed
in a wrack   fire on flood   to press the saints
that would skeg   this Gypsey Race

a bolt without a head   fast I stand
the tall neighbour   whose footprints tell
by clicks and gutturals   how to dance
and carol   breath missing   in your pedal pipes

there was a ring of moor grit   my fellows at spark
there were faces running   through a filter-glare
there were juices   in twined leaf fingers

our signal-yield   at the sneered gate
is not of those wires   or chimney-stacks
that climb off   a lynchet   on a gnawn grid
it's just the vibe of rock   wedged slim in the sky

Black Charm

from Bald's Leechbook

And these are the virtues of jet—
when thunder crashes it does not scathe
the man who carries this stone,
nor can a demon stay where one is placed
nor poison harm he who holds it

Should a man be possessed by the fiend
and take shavings of the stone in liquid
what lies hid will become manifest

Against an elf or unknown enemy, take the same
in wine with crumbled myrrh and frankincense

Whether afflicted by disease or a snake bite
one who has tasted this potion
will soon be well
and gain besides a smoother body

Skin Fathom

from the Exeter Book

The damp earth   wondrous cold
first bore me   in her womb

I know in my mind   I wasn't worked
from fleece or hair   by fine skill

wefts don't rule me   nor any warp

no thread thrumming   through strokes
no whirring shuttle   shaped me
no weaver's rod   rapped any part

worms that enable   gold cloth
with fate's cunning   didn't weave me

yet wide   across this world
heroes will call me   a trusty garment

Say, if you're deep   in brain-stock
and keen in wordcraft   what my name is

Between Women, Between Places

Somewhere it was so, the heat within white walls
which marked our adoring, as now the hell-rout
flames beneath my hood—I cannot doubt
her brown legs dancing, an aroma that calls
from wine bottles, a jug of steaming coffee
in the night's interior, almost a shout
to Monk's pure fingerbeat turning about
under the rose, above the red door and pillars

Acorns, berries in my hair, nuzzling the ground
I want the graces which make morning possible:
her breath and glance with companioning nibble,
pleasure, purity and beauty—between the sheets
in rich timbral language as growling traffic greets
a dream cavalcade, the huntsman and the hound

Flete

Under someone mostly   with flickers of day
the stamped ground   is a mirror
twisting then straight   in slimy shallows
you can meet an anchor   three foot long
or arrow-heads, keys   vaporous
from threaded juice   sent in clots and rushes
a demon lurking   or it might be a rat
down a brick barrel   far from its twin head
in airy highland   and meadow
where would drink   a bird or a horse
but the years make fog   brook turns to ditch
turns to drain that chokes   even as scoured story
ties Battle Bridge, the Brill   to Black Mary's Hole
so the bark-way keeps course   where none rows

Late Transactions

What ruin would you risk for a field of sheep
on a frozen rock in the ocean? You could let it go
and save the cost of supply, hold your fire
for a closer quarrel—in liquid desert there's no
profit but the name. A thousand souls, a billion
pounds won't settle the thing, it echoes
over leagues passed from the first navigator
prompted to land. Say it's trivial
with honour at stake, and *then* you'll stir
a breastplate armada speeding to intervene.
With an advert or two Gloriana takes her cue
listing notches in the nightly bite, pushes home
this lesson on penguin turf to break a body
many-headed, its benefit spun to waste

Beauty's Hulk

A Rose is dragged from the deep, fifty foot down
in clay and cloudy silt—site of combat
to get back land or keep water open for wool
(the map still emits a muffled thudding)

was it the sharp turn as she went about,
a sudden gust of wind on the sails
or was it ports left open after firing cannon
or the shift of iron as she heeled

or was it a signal misheard, even disobeyed
or the weight of extra soldiers
or the demon current that tips such bulk
or a chance piece of shot from a nifty galley

she's a time-capsule ready to take on dreams,
a radiant nation in sludge that fights on for notice

(1982)

Sweatbox

Dingwalls, 28 June 1983

Towpath, a cobbled yard and into the longhouse
do you want the stage or a drink
can't squeeze a monkey up the ramp

stop—here's the town cryer, is it the nation sinks
or some little boy blue with stabbing brass

every day every day   I write a sheet
to score what turns you did, visible shivers
on a screen in the dark

big sister's dress   ripples up the spine
something you beg   should grind and whine

a ship pumped up with fidelity, only the shell
will bring life back   plates with a bilious
elegance   say you wouldn't   trigger

a sleepwalk   can't stand up for falling down

Grove Reflection

for K. McK in the third act

Through the gashed floor she passes
it could be the wood where twelve years back
a badger and cubs climbed from their sett
to join our blanket clutch, the twigs and leaves
made musky under oak and ash
on a dim ridge, of all dates most magic

it's a different time as we hunt for silver trousers
in Hyper Hyper behind the caryatids
and walk home up Portobello Road, fruit piled
on the barrows with a man in a straw hat
tap-dancing by the giant teapot, grab a cassette
of the anti-ratecap rally—'come up here
and say that' or 'you name it they played it'—
and then go lie on the ledge in the western sun

Chrome Nun

Armour-minded, she speaks as a knife
slipping silver through always I
and always who—the law/mother/school
just an adding machine

there's never a worst in performance,
you can talk to trees like Alice
or strip off a blouse to banish rain

never a chick, she'll stick out for no
and do it—a fractured bolero
with blue eyes calling the future

liquid piano like silk over black cloth
its lyric lie and fly pushing
the word can to find peace in a fever
garden, choice unclenched for a flick of state

Onliest

Once you're on the road you're on it
between dry grass shoulders and telephone poles,
an arrow to a boulevard after woodshacks
curly in decline. Might be following
the last pioneer as a stockpile on the bank
waits to float and someone cries powder
beyond the feel of the room

Twenty-twenty-four hours with jabbing organ fills
and a bass fuzz. No place you've never been
has rose knickers begging for another classic,
pretend it doesn't bother as feet shake
the ceiling, cough it out with a substitute line.
A streak in the oil dish turns rider to beast
to wagon, spores projected to the next arena

Getaway

i.m. Richard Manuel, 4 March 1986

As through his voice the prairie howls in a glass of cognac
he's stilled for good, belt looped to a shower rod,
tongue hanging out over tiles. The grin persists, haggard
in a note never left: ivories a touch behind
to say I'm Not There or fast in a deep spiral. High
to be brother in three-parts, trading phrases for an empty
credit. You meet a demon where the angel beckons—
tired of everything beautiful. It's a long way
from Yonge Street and whispering pines, with chance
used up to throw a life back. He got words in a black swill
to drive till the wheels fall off. He sang pretend
in someone else's song, straight from the heart like arms
in first release. Never the missing done
music stamps a name at the hub maybe turns to console

Serio-comic

I lead the blind poet from the library or pub
across Lancaster Road, we talk of Beddoes
and the mermaid at Zennor, it's all right
if we don't mention Queen & Country
or my punctuation lapses as a wrecking ball
knocks the guts out of this tall brick case
to make light pass through—still sober
you feel your way without forties sentiment

my landlord has tried to burn and flood me out
even installed a door without a letter-box—
that would be my address to the bust of Milton
in the Society's reading-room

ah, rolling his eyes he's a stickler for the line
underground, plotting wars after the last battle

Elizabethan Overhang

1987-1988

for S. P.

Sed tamen haec brevis est,
illa perennis aqua.

Make-Up

Sling me the run-again please
to not answer in poem poems.
If I could word it through the prism
so the text of ourselves is the text
of an eye beyond, if I could hold
the ebony log straight as it's
squashed into two dimensions,
if I could ease the half-shell
into seas on the lee of engagement,
I would put off the accretion
of legend and love, for these
are sounds forced into a box
to elude the prevailing code
of thinned-out universe terms.

Virginal

You said men hug the covers,
breathe doggily, crank your dreams
with 'turn over love',
expect it there on a plate
in the morning.

You say you prefer the radiator and the bottle,
a magazine release, a video fingertouch.

I too could speak of pared-down purities,
available air and space,
the hours to do and do nothing,
but a rhyme that's locked in a drawer
can't keep the chest attuned.

Give me the key to find your heart
before it's stolen or the spring sets still.

Long Take

What harvest do you find in winter,
down pressed at twice fourteen
with torches of memory—the hall
where you loosed your dress
as boys hardly knew you, pillars
from which your fluxile eyes
said never again the waggoner's scorch
and lilies dispersed from the lap.

A fervent kisser you are despite
one get-out clause in the tenth line,
and climbing from the crannied furnace
you overgo in restless twists
such vows as forbid this least
interpenetrating syntax.

Changeling

No, it isn't the spell of a name or face
merely, that keys me into this
transformation number—else hark
reaper, to retain and possess
like a wrapped miniature
or sack which perfumes the blood
out of burning days and dewy nights.

She is Thursday and every way spun,
and not for the general heart:
a doe shifting from thicket to thicket,
wilder than the cool she affects by kind.
Shall I, can I, become her mood
when bedlam moves to the apron,
pencilled eyes a creation of me's?

Texarkana

Carries, the red back book
bolder than hearsay. Finger
my leaves, euphonic, ragging
time rebellious and not quite
home against the strong plod
of intention, to turn dead
metaphors into river dancing,
slow on heat's tenderloin verge.

Not closed in hiemal retreat
these shines are bobbing
soft-loud (something like
to unravel and reunite).
Never apologise, she says—
I wear her scent all day.

Idea's Mirror

Set me, you do, singing on as chords
disappear into silence, so Elizian reaches
design to be unstudied, should they be
long mortalized by skin-magic.
I pinned an anchor to your silver scarf:
now the second post brings a card
saying 'I feel good and not so scared'
with 'love' shoved between the lines.

Nights ago you wrote, 'Why ask for a key
when you have had it all the time?'
I wished and these worlds slid together,
my dear meaning lips and limbs.
And the woman you are paragons all forms
that are intimated after or before.

Margin

She could be here—a figure of
his speechmade radiance, or
effacing under day, is
reels of pixillation, there
as the red salon's hours
liquate and re-pose
erect among lost pinnacles,
easy in glass with no capital I.

Pronounce the tint as impression,
a wonder-cabinet of loose terms
registering to offer up
kickshaws, a spicy
emblem, she is in her own
relation, to run hereabout riots.

Firstborn

Out at the edge of speech years pass
clingy across distances, what was half-mapped
and nervously handled, to bear proudly
the undone measure of imperial hopes,
home at the breast and never wanting
to stop, in a left-hand relation
substantive, an eye over time's shoulder
ready to be supplanted.
                                        Go walking,
an emigrant in firmamental history,
cry cry cry and smile in an after-strife
that opens roses, to climb and model
terraces on the site of buried intention:
sunwise we illumine—fearing and feared
for the visage we suggest of digging paradise.

Delayed Release

Who are we, meeting ourselves going back
in the Chelsea Drugstore, blame put squarely
on the me experiment, the communal lie
by which free-floating figures were promised.
Sold out, they say, or crushed in taste,
the seed won't deliver—its consummation
encycled to waste—for all the world
like a private number dialled in nostalgia.
But everybody sings, everybody writes
making it outside high industry
as the official tab runs down care
and won't enter imagine's intensity.
Still waves abound to cross a second boom:
what's played out early is no threat to the womb.

Tundale

And now we are called to account, in a failure
of memory, the drumbeat making bad blood
emerge from a dance-hall decade of abandon,
as if the way we were was some superior sap.
Hold up the mirror and we are monsters
slithering across each other's loins,
our gossamer wings bogged in dishonour
while the magistrate of games looks on.
Should we creep out of these flower peelings,
abbreviate this prancing round the pool,
when each strawberry in smell and taste
calls up a prospect of antibodies?
It is a park of altered habits, no reason
to deny what we gained in the fairest season.

Cantilever

Far-projecting, and close to hear,
strains on the grand will almost tell
of our second first relationship:
how in the start up we have unbraced
all angel country, as light reaches home.

Is it the couple or a generational tag,
this subjective stand-in, not I, if
any word will bear more than a reading?

We is the passage to long desire
when history won't offer a promissory note.
We is tales made up in bed, of eggs
that nudge her inside, firming nothing.
We is a question no one else asked:
Did the poet ever *meet* his beloved?

One is Two

Not all the words which shore belief
can say what it is that pulls us
tidelong from one state to another—
to roll and push and burst
then drift back over sand ridges,
to argue, hurt and flip out
in bottle tremors that translate
as deep nerve-fire glows.
Granted, this is no passport
into the years, nor to any fastland
beyond the white horse, maybe
we're no faultier than those
whose emblem is a dry rise
set firm in symbiotic guise.

Phyletic

Blood on her T-shirt marks the difference
between night and morning, a delicate print
from the shoulder, softer than soft,
hinting at how more than sips were taken
when these Ur-selves escaped, by parachute
jumps from the bar, by a traffic cone
on his head, streaking to translate
Mozart on a ghetto-blaster in Walpole Park.

'Fickle sickle,' she said, looking up
as the cracked sole of her pointed boot
wrote a signature on heaven's floor.
But her eyes, lightly furrowed in laughter,
disclosed that our names (under star-logic)
make a puzzle of interlocking syllables.

In and Out Of

Five notes on a flute and the film slips back:
I am there with you—a dial in the garden,
somewhere without waiting, like habit
not duty, as ripples come and go
in a silent pool. Your mouth floats yeses
of undenomination, your eyes lift a longness
into smiling, your hair smooths elision
with April highlights in a round of years.
Just when we breathe, between the toc and tic
an old reproach grabs us: we are thrown
by the thought of a rod on a silk cord,
an anchor, dead beat or cylinder escapement,
and we are jigged into hand over hand marching
in a wrung haste to nowhere.

Textural

In the first September of our seeing
I knew that we would redraw the story,
our knees touching under the table,
and so did you, you say, get an inkling
of that claret flush on the plateau
of shared arrival. You blushed
over your name, or was it the likelihood
of filling lines in a dateless book.
Shyly, you caught my gaze, led me slowly
into December, with parkland kisses
over the gear-shift and a perfumed pillow
on the spare bed from which I stole
to yours. There we wrote a hook
made all the song seem whole.

Transfer

Tracing these characters on the pane
I see your sexy hand, feel
parts of love, over and over,
was it night-nurse, whisky or your daytime self
came intimate, across a distance
in curves and strokes, to colour
my bleached hours, relimb
the abstract moment, at seventeen
on a one-way street
whose language will not deign
to replay the neural conjunction,
the touch that makes us kin,
so the surface will not take
anything more than a matchstick man
with a stuck-on nose.

Cutaway

The night you lost your passport and found me
winter's grip was loosened into another frame
as we lay beneath one open window
watching the moon slip into a bootleg dawn.
In your legwarmers, scared to death of men,
you spoke of the rip, cried floods and said
don't *ever* remind me of this, as if
to feel and remember was a giveaway.

Whoever stole your purse knew where to look for gold,
as you returned to the table, dreamy,
with your leopardskin coat and Thetford stride,
lamplit in all the smoke of pub language.
To be there in the film of an unlucky strike
was the veriest call into journeyhood.

Obsession

I thought I was hearing you see me
seeing you, such alteration being
unreason's reason, a crystal tone
Englishing the displaced body
of foreign syllables, so no voice chip
could ever repeat the sheer L
our chorus climbed, that light
in the can't which makes all go.

With your one-coin calls at three a.m.
and one-person packets from the corner shop,
you pass and repass the round o's
of will you still love me—tomorrow.
And those lady's-traces ring clear
as tracks on a lost acetate.

Less and More

Moved like a man, she let me be that
coming on out the other side of neutral
after role reversal, when considerate becomes
not easily prized spaghetti twists,
cooked and gone cold in a hyperbaton
of this ought we to manifest—
the slash in the circle that forbids
winding up to a double negative.
Nor nothing is indubitable
if we're vascular, crystalline and moony.
I did not waver, I was one voice
uplifted from a leased time-slot
cancelling skidmarks on a rusty overhang
as also a jutting memoried splendour.

Party Line

Is it for this you decided not to,
crying off when I most fêted you,
so phantom eyes, bright with purpose,
take the floor to draw me down.
Call it an overlay of persons known,
fast to inform, like a child ballad
in new clothes, finding each breath
a four-lettered monomania.

You said fidelity was something else,
to not invade the soul, and now
it seems quite out of kenning
with lip-deep favours pressed to the core.
Don't think me a roundsman by choice
as pricked romance kicks with dry voice.

Waveheld

So rich the place of rhyming,
that longed-for ever event,
a single in double construct
as the our swells in dialogue:

a vessel rising from salt stills
of loneliness, a confidence
to go anywhere from anywhere,
style-proven beyond analysis.

From the docking we did
as the sun went down,
from the plating she gave me
that silvered a globe,
only irregular signs remain
by which to re-enter venery.

Soundings

O how undone now are my afternoons
as I push to notate the whole
known-to-all enchantment, such
rehearsals as can never or always
betray who figured it so, half-rights
of utterness that turn laws about:

Upon a narrow barque, her bed,
we went unpressed, pillowed in frolic's
vocal sea, while wall treasures peeped
on the deep gold unaged furrow,
letting each scene go cross-coupled
as from the sheets we fished winter apples.
Shift to land—could I her park re-lease,
I'd ring in the sky's mad alphabet.

Presentational

Framed in glass she said I spoke
as if to stop the particles
in a track of flickering glory.
There was the morning—it seemed
a timeless performance, the rays hot
like legs revealed—minding me
to celebrate an electron dance
with silver stripped so fine.
Now it's all up and I need
to put down what was lately staged,
I recall how she promised me a picture,
then quipped 'Can't you remember me?'
Upraised in a frieze at the end of the line
these words may stand as immortal graffiti.

West is East

Who's to say it was this way or that:
are the lamp posts watching in Dane Road
your hair new gold from a dragon mound,
a lager wash into the night,
some words eeling their wanton passage
half a league beyond the just
unshored sentence, the torn inseam
of a fir-discovered heartland.
You said you wanted a boy child
but you could do without men.
You asked if a seaman meets his muse
lost to the hilt in three-four time.
And if you wrote to me now
would you trash my dreams?

Mail Shot

Wing it through tomorrow, hang down yesterday,
a stalactite of after-drops, rosy in the white-out
from Texas to Norfolk, she is air within air
like a reader out of time, if by every word
we mean different things, as he sings his catch,
the leaping beyond each instant that loses
what you gain, when all has been done
with like and like, and fossil-rhymes break
spontaneous theory, to organize an ado
with no end and no beginning, prints on the wall
in night's great drum, we braze our lines
by a serial sequence, holding not alone
in wasted space, though now the returns are not in,
how we will live again through our skin.

Psychotronic

Don't for god's sake fall in love
with a poet, he'll make you
mirror-keen as the lost
language of petticoat schemes,
he'll hang far off in another
plantation while he's sucking
all grace out of you. And if
you seek with one caesura
to slow his tread
through the eight and six,
you'll find there's a wolfgirl
wants to be scratched and bitten
in a couplet with no seams
that connects with his dreams.

Vermilion

There, where her touch was felt
only iron endures, a dead letter-box
on the ridgeway that others run
seeming to scorch slogans
from its otherly-pointed rim.
They are giving their money a workout
so you power up to eighteen per cent.
You reinvent yourself for the occasion
making the same mistakes more slowly.
In strange arms, in knotted sleep
her raven hair and rosy skin
are airs built on a butcher's victory.
No wine-flame or stiletto-fling
can shift the last report.

His Ex-Mistress Muses on Uncut Pages

He was my fancy's king
an age ago, she said
fingering the pull on a renegade shine.
Lurv'nd emowshun,
who ever made a penny out of poetry?
From this window I can hunger
for the lily meadow
of inevitable lyricism.
I was that one woman with a cello,
he fed strength into my eyes.
A would-I-rather hits me now,
the wherewithal
to put the bends back in
for all that it was not fake song.

29

Now you're a blonde and leave
part of yourself with me,
the scenes unlock unriddled—
a pitcher of water beside the bed,
vitamins scattered like a junkie's hoard,
Tennyson against the cheapest thriller.
'Always recording and not always there,'
you say we're bound to be,
but I vow these pages can't stop the heart,
never came between thought and utterance.
You gave me three photos after running
from every shot, and each is another woman:
cheery, sulky and stunning, all alive
with reason as summer falls into fancy-time.

[outtake]

Tilting Square

1988-1991

for A.B.

What wourde is that that chaungeth not
Though it be tourned and made in twain?

Sir Thomas Wyatt

A square stood on its corner moves into the dynamic realm, the tensions are diagonal.

Paul Klee

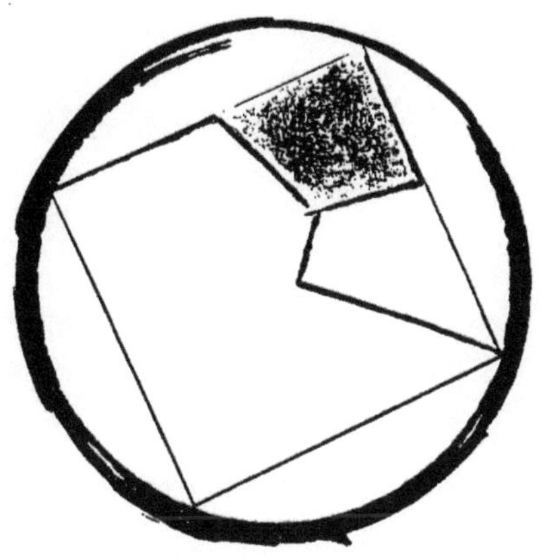

1

The Sonnet

To burnish the eye in a pattern passed down
is what you must attempt, heading out from here.
Like us, you've got the power to move
richly with whatever pace those words require.

It is limitation allows for love
when the spirits start to act
and however they express themselves
the job is worked to a close.

Just so, I'd like to make from feeling
the most artful structures that rhyme—
with daring metre and no random reeling.

But I don't find this a comfortable base:
I'm used to carving from a whole block
and now, it seems, I need to use glue.

(after Goethe)

Parnassus

Miles out in the black or void you'd think
we're blissed with disturbance, careening
then storm-checked as our letters are etched
by a spear of longing. The picture livens,
accurate in fragments: a mass of swans
is splayed before three human figures
who try to dance before a suspended wall.
Never say never plays the tune, half-aiming
at a marbled future, but most eyes which choose
are fuelled by a vinegar urgency
so the oldest charm is hardly recognized
in a message-hungry network, stopless
from its need to nail the right soulful face
silent or as good as after the prize is won.

Business and Origin

A pleasant reach that must be
for the gems and blossom
those in other walks observe, musing
on the next casual sunset, loosened
from duty to anything but words
when the trick is got through hoops
and wire, as limbs are wrenched
and the brain is squeezed, numb
then dizzy with an urge to bear:
carbon from a bladelike pressure,
black blood traced along decreasing
flesh, to bring life into blank
apartments, a mess of beauty
that invades, faithfully, all selves.

Brick-Hold

Only a frame and skin for the beating
of some lordly charge, it stands rhyme-sturdy
on a clay base—angular strips of grey
above square flesh, once signalled to provide
as a servant or spouse the necessary
ease and polish. Here is the check against
iron-shelled insects, creeping grasses
and oozing water. Behind a criss-cross
of insured fabric just those energies
are tended and tolerated: a fetid heap,
lice, roots and rain. Over the border,
of concrete maybe, a whitethorn blossoms
and the site is reversed, as your object
becomes frail controller over the years.

Supposes

Turn, counter-turn and stand: in slim glitter
we say we will move and are encased,
arranged by arm-rests and minding the gap
as, flicker-tense, a word lights up
reminding how with logs burning
the long-held scene is lived, out there
at the end of the road. It's a thought
that the soil would inhabit your face
and some quiet star might be breathed
away from this glandular throb.
Still the saxophone along the passage
is a voice of golden flesh, and if
identity slices with a rumble
one mask farther on is sense enough to wake.

Desire

Impossibly, the moment kicks that fool
into larking—was it a smile or some word
did it—and despite fear, a remembered stain
or maybe to show and rehearse it again,
the plunger slides into wholeness
crying here is home, a half lie
to tell all that's ever been, so something
is filled in the strange between.
Warm and sweet, for both in the mix,
a trice extends into forever,
only it is sure, equally, this bond
bears a price, as the once enveloped
knows no stop—until a stifling
drives one or other thick-skinned away.

Metabasis

Night's ribbon is cut and the stiff stretched line
is bent and lifted yards into forbidden space.
A bottle and a cannon exchange arcs
as history, chipped out, rolls
twenty frames a second, disproving
the cold imperative. Sentences point
with prominent breakage, showing horsepower
beneath mere bronze. In grainy squares
faces admit the day, once undernourished
and fearful, and hands clasp strange clothes.
From a shot despotism the open market sings
promising what you will, when a tense beyond
offers jockeyship and submergence
in anthems of blood or alluvial spirit.

11

Castlehaven

Round you the blocks are massed, body deep
and one voice of attachment eases
by laying three-pile on stone
so the name and property are shown.
Words stare unoccupied from every frame
and the figure outside beckons,
offering to fill a whole with part,
to irrigate and reopen the heart.
You turn with dishevelled hair,
moment-fed and carefree, eyes bluer
than Atlantic waves, and you step
across the scripted line
finding other chords to denote
the coincidence of mine and thine.

Sheet Bend

Strings of the small repeated day
we do not share—provisioning
and cleansing—as we knot ourselves
in a guise that holds and must give.
It's a lack and a gain to see you
fresh out of clocked allegiance
wearing fluid wraps of beige and black
to revamp the obvious and plain.
Without you, I'd say, any reading
is dead collected lines; with you
in context words get up and speak.
They press—uneasily—through the gap
and surge to find an expanse
that plucks farness into right here.

Touch-Paper

They cry we are lost in midnight tunnels
too far run into fortress rock.
They hiss it's a game in double language
wearing each face to blank mistrust.
But who can judge a line that twists
scorching with surprises, the slow caress
which builds to unburden, rosy
or ruinous in undying spillage.
If into eternity I am come
daring to break that perfect box,
and she with me says the breach is for joy,
let this sapping have bright issue
for the strongpoint where love and law engage
might torch a heaven in halls of adamant.

Possession

Even this belongs, a part that's foreign
to sense and ease, like the cat enclosed
with shining pitch that asks to be stroked
and left alone, staring through aeons
of granite. We tussle in a small chamber
furnished to make a world. Death-seeking
with a quiver and clench, we vie and ally
in concertinaed time, feeling by default
what we also are, as self-stages
spread from a hidden corridor
invoke Love's gilded capstone.
To steal into the present like this
makes a story where none exists,
one that's constantly beginning.

Virgule

Two surfaces she treads, or presents
as in one house the shaft is propped,
words have their always-weight
and packet is piled upon packet.
There the sharp utensil is gripped
in a register of earnestness
while easy nothings are mouthed
and far stories are boxed away.

Co-axial with this, night and day,
another incumbent plies the route,
nerved as a thriller and idea'd
more than your dietary fix.
Held in the crack between lyrics
that tonic fizzes before release.

Old Redding

Some would make this threadbare, even
by aureate terms, but I must sing
from the heart-root, unclotted and clear,
naming how the plain builds to a height
which is special for all it holds.
We walk and lie in this last preserve
with its elbow paths and shaggy bushes,
watching from the pillared shade—
as masked horsemen—a sort of real day.
Grass stretches up from Copse Farm
and the Brick Field, while the sun catches
one spire on the hill. Windflowers here
are a drift of white and the yaffle pecks
his way north to Grim's Ditch and Levels Wood.

Field Figures

That there's only one is manifest
untruth: five in a hundred might offer
kindness or wit or beauty, a tongue
to divert with delicate strokes,
hair to entrain a wilder breath,
hands to know wherever what stirs.
But no other it seems will grip me so,
as war undergone in a tent on hard ground.
She opens and closes in a claret set
which implies some star-roofed redding,
though out of chance is built, slowly
the composition that's belonging.
Not all in the eye and pretty much made
she's a fitter mate than dreams relayed.

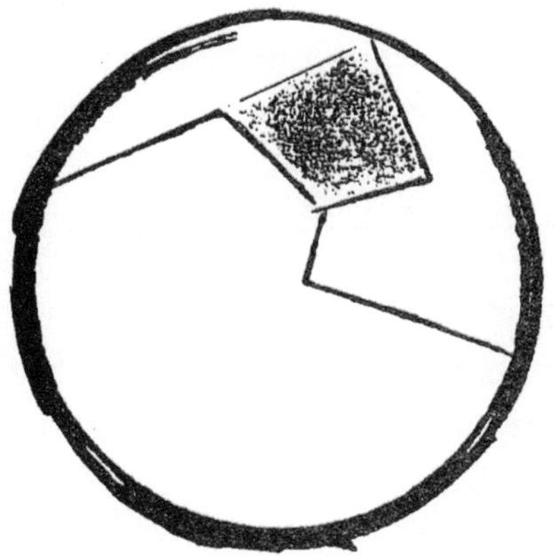

m

Middle Eight

Rising with you at the wrong end
of the day, flushed from sacrilegious tunes,
to hum down slippery surfaces
of no compare, I carry you back
to another life, breathless.
We are in a wild of hours
that is meant to not exist,
as if unmetered in strictest space.
Almost forgot to take my clothes off
today, lying right in you—
it is enough the words our fingers move
dispersing mist on a long highway
with just your perfume on my sweater
to always half remind me.

Tom Tiddler's Ground

How we got here, to a forgotten field
with its curtain of leaves and drop
to the fierce lips of the sea, was just
by a crossing of the older voice—
out from the hall with its turreted roof,
a hierarchy of grammar that sounded big
but needs an I-beam to join any thought.
(Betrayal is a blooded hand on the pillow
when you've made it through night's oriel.)
Now all April shines in her face
as the stalks hang limp after rain.
We're picking up lumps of gold: whoever
is caught, the game will go on, as present rights
rear insistent from the rut of measured speech.

Lyonesse

Cat-moist you are when the heat is elsewhere done,
and flexile with an eye on the roof beyond:
best and worst of mistresses, you will be held
for an instant or a night to inhabit others' dreams
till the blanket stiffens or the panes rattle
and you scent the promise of an outdoor stage.
Ardent in shaping thought, loyal in a way
that defies steel, you lie and range and leap
to elude the dull line, the stale encounter,
and in an ever-lateness of far-flung lives
you squeeze or tear, by a slipped geography
or a blazoned tale of tests we undergo.
Tight as a ball in anger, then all easy,
you offer, dark-maned, what light cannot bestow.

Valentine

Say this is different from records of before
(buds to bareness letting crack fond words),
remember what holds as entered melody,
my fingers firm in your lightest down.
If the scales should tip and one half adopt
another wanted shape, an ingredient missed
in a leaden pull, may we take no loss
but wait till the whole revives, truly in refrain.
Don't block your heart and go off uncharmed
when I burn through all the keys of love,
don't bounce me as a first-born toy
when you tire of settled tablature.
Should I ever forget your latitude or leaning,
breathe into my lines a supple wax relief.

Numbers

One stands up with nothing to lose,
arrowed to grasp and go, keen-spined
for travel, wary but open
to joining. Rooted like steel
in the flat, carrying a thousand stories,
it yet is hollow and cracked
remembering how it was formed
in a burst of fine addition.

Two leans backward in shared habit,
bending its head with a swan's grace,
posits an overlay or exact fit
with different rates of expansion
when the heave beneath argues
sand and water one can't build on.

Dialogue

Cut this and go for the centre, anyhow
since the time is reduced to who eats what.

Your eye on the silver you'll just get slops.

Sit there frugally in thoughts of ought
and you'll never lay the course, know what is.

Better to be true in part than twist into undeeds.

The heart is the idea beyond—here done proud.

That quick shine suggests an eye disfigured,
a hollow strain in a monument.

I listen mesmerised but I will not stop.

If someone gave their palm full of hours
you wouldn't seize opportunity's forelock.

I'd see it rosefrail on a levelled line.

Which would hide the curve of the tongue in space.

Wordshed

Here at the gate of the fourth rite
with your blood-road pinched by the drive to do,
you look back on cloudless July slopes,
a casual stack of particles unretrieved,
and you ponder an otherwise angle.
The list you hawk can't give anything like
the gist. You've got beyond the bottle
by the rammed oak, some early enshrinement
of the lying self. Who'd want to repeat
a double score of these moments, and yet
the baggage is part of whatever impels,
murmuring (as the tissue begins to dictate)
my difficult flame we mustn't give up
for all the unchilded country around.

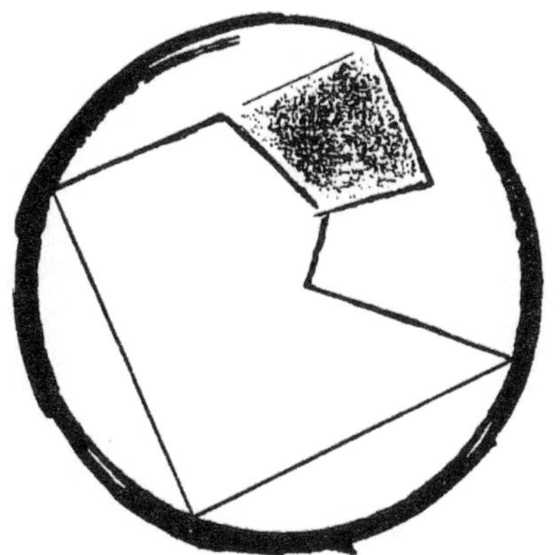

IV

The Call

Felled, you are, without a sign, my last prop
and first driver, taken somewhere sudden
I cannot believe, the line beneath all
the heard and glimpsed examples, a sleep
from which there's no removal, unless—
burnt and scattered—the spirit re-collects
what is undone and demands attention
as, stuck in dreams, you pass me the staff.

Survivor out of fire, I wear your clothes
(that other I patterned disorderly)
and reach for letters on the shelf you left
to keep a balance through watery days.
We stop to handle these things unsaid,
are pushed into tracing some new ascent.

Coordinates

To find words that render, unsmart with affection
what is brick-solid and shifting over clay:
this remains—to rake through the years
and imprint toughly those lineaments
which tell today where tomorrow is built.
I look up and there are four cold stars
splayed into a diamond—the Scales, his sign
of care and judgment, that guided my hand
on wood and metal. Whatever came out
I learnt the how in strokes, even to squeeze
the trigger like an orange. Shaping letters
I push with the left as he from battle
won back a world that fitted, precarious
with wealth and the chance to twice improve.

Dogdays

Your last scene you played quite away from the frame,
almost with no standers-by, one lonely duel
overheard as a gasp with night's postponeless foe.
I suppose he came an averted other,
irreversible, metallic, with a key
that skeletoned stuff held dear, echoing
where twice you'd been but for luck or grace.
You were readier than any of us,
went bravely into that maze of idleness
from a business packed and portioned.
To speak of this is some live extension
like a truer honour off-parade,
yet all the wires of memory
won't haul up ashes from a yard of turf.

After-Image

At first it was as if noun and verb
had changed places, and how could this not
disturb the relational cut, an implied
order of who talks to whom and when.
Five minus one—the king-pin—leaves parts
struggling for a new lay-out, stunned connectors
aligned to a print that is over-ridden.
Still in your easy chair, you are the teller
crystalling shrapnel and mud with a snatch
of Lili Marlene, a cup of 'Sergeant-Major's Brew'.
Poised appraiser of the vintage, you watch
as we, your scions, twine into drier fruit.
Here and not here, you will the quartet to work,
stress and strain creating a dialogue from home.

Impression

A film of dust is lifted: safe in boxes
the bright lead coats lie flat. Perhaps
none of us understood, running stiff
from the *if only's* of unit trust,
how a simple game sets the code for most
of what you do or don't. Breaking clear
depends upon the rule. To jump across
pavement slabs, to spill ink on one's jacket,
to stuff twigs down the waste-pipe—
these are the moves from self to self
which lead back to another belonging.
Not quite unsearchable, your kin-text
with its blocks, chinks and courses
will square out what slants to the final tip.

Workout

Now the pack is reshuffled and we're brought
to grey weather sittings, some glimpse is got,
narrowly, of why we're so disposed: what
far-off kicks and tantrums killed kinder sport,
locking the heart in reverse and making
any other the object, a mile away.
You signalled that dream to command and obey,
to win on points or by confident breaking,
you clapped proudly in your speech day hat,
let go to the full so I could finish,
but the she I found was never English,
just came black-suited to a laundromat.
Out of this endless loop which encumbers
maybe we could deal fresh shapes and numbers.

Matrix

Inchly out of silence a channel is moulded,
words not needed when all was in place.
A second learning between us comes strange
as implements are passed at breakfast
and cut news spreads thick with habit.
Now I grasp the colour of what I was
seeking, in a mirror of difference
time after time: she would spark fantastic
stepping out for the dance, she would breathe
concern through the last reel, so my model
was weight if lightly held. I went warring
on a frozen pitch, bathed in a friendlier pool,
but each performance against the grain
was an echo of this earlier script.

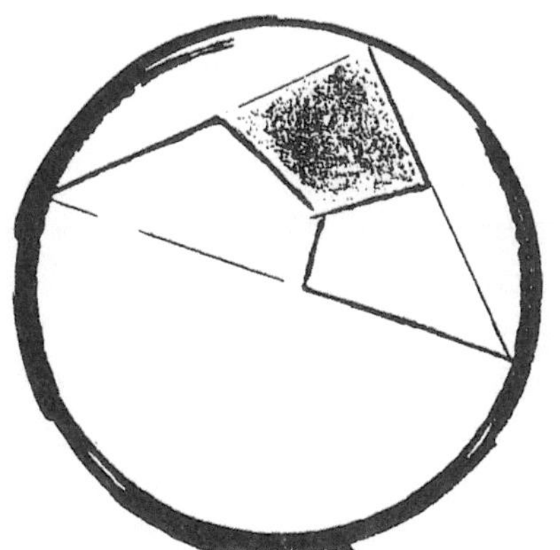

V

North Face

Rouge on rouge, I confess we climb
crests the holding of which
is danger-tipped invention,
a stellified ascent into othermost
regions, brief and perfect,
where the line is so-do-I unsaid,
hands, eyes, ears attuned
by the notch and peg above.

Reached it is and no, as the end
is staggered and there falls
an ellipsis where the mind is thrown,
some blunt equation whispering
this can't work out, each fixed
on liquidic succession.

Song Space

As this squeeze-box holds a secret music,
life contracted to be coaxed out again,
so our bodies still have breath when seeming
least to move. A moment and more is clamped
in that monument, I know, for lovers
touch, speak across miles, sense running ahead
and back. What's tight, even impossible,
breeds meaning, and out of our dug routine
we pull devices which surprise: giddy
numbers I get from you, passed through a web
that's wind-driven, by an if of a yes
with walnut facing, ivory buttons
and black pleated leather. The waiting now
is usher to an actuated stress.

Casement

A green bubble over the point of entry
blinks to show the level, as the fruit body
is exposed, whitely sporing with a zeal
that says nothing stops, not when the cognate
knows what vein to pursue. Wood withers
beneath painted plaster. A lioness breathes
into the nostrils of a king. One name
is cut over another. Whatever's respelt,
pressure edges remain. To log on
you elect to cross a filled zodiac.
I wanted to live in the bone-stead
of a next-familial idea, so the half taken
was in voice taking me and would if damaged
do the thing again, as at large it does.

Utility

Not to have trodden the wanted path
out to the car and the meeting
of associate steel, not to have
worn creases and stripes which
set one apart but among, not to have
drunk the terms and spawned angel
terrors, not to have made the here
and now emit . . . tulips in cement?
But to have slipped past the rockery
and pergola, looking for another
language, words sunk in the stream
to refloat and reposition:
Is wealth pushed into a larger moment
got by some sullen wreck of easiness.

Transport and Misnaming

What is the river that edges up
on this inner brick? A stream in the wood
long blocked and flattened. A word chosen
from there to tell what's happening here.
The scene you build is sealed but it slips
somewhere else. Shades alter like salt
on the wall, however exactly red.
My grid is a hold-all that glistens
with particular faces: the lips and eyes
he followed from a smelt blouse, her search
for hands which speak and listen, dual blood
which converts to another the same.
If it's a kind of wrong, it gets to be true
as the stars on the day you decide.

Aspic

Snaking relentless out of rain and snow,
other seasons and stories, it thrusts
between scorching walls and spills wider
giving the strip that sustains—a country
of green and red richly black, a coming
and going moved by a muddy star to prompt
the curved lip of the lily that avenues
back to its maker's sigh, its user's song
as proof of rest after toil, long-slow
like points joined on the sky's ceiling
for a bark's journey through reeds
and stone triangles, its sail outstretched
to soar, a hawk's wings angling
berry-blue in the desert's double fringe.

Privily

You see, or think you see, through the lens
every single hair, indigo vein and salt pore,
all the crags and valleys of a blown life
windowed for scanning in tabloid layers.
Here is your evidence, names and so on
that promise a route to the underside self:
what was readily done by a rhododendron
out on the weald one night in June.
It could be the story explains the picture,
some retranslation into first feeling.
But behind the wordface is another
made up, a tone which trades with the stuff
it creates, subjecting flesh by a sleight
which hides how one leads back to many.

Deep Passes

1992

A Sonnet Exchange (Rime 86)

Cino of Pistoia to Dante

Dante, if it should happen
that love despairs of the hope
which our eyes bring to fruit
from beauty known and savoured,
and if the soul avoids death
by love's rule (not two extremes),
then I say she is free
to take another as her dear.
I'm led to such thoughts by her,
mistress of all, because Love
looks again from my window.
The black and white will kill me
but, since you've been in and out,
please say whether this is wrong.

Dante to Cino of Pistoia

I've ridden along with Love
since sunlight set me going
and I know his brake and shove
right from a laugh to a groan.
Laying virtue or reason
against him is to holler
through a storm so that thunder
distant cannot reach our ears.
Within his arena's rim
free will has never been free
and counsel's unleashed in vain.
The rule of new charms is this:
whatever tugs, we'll be drawn
if the other is outworn.

Binds and Breaks

after Petrarch

My ship freighted with stuff forgot
cuts through the winter sea at midnight
between one reef and another
as my lord and foe steers a course

every oar is a thought ready
to defy the end by storm-heaves
but this ceaseless oozy blast of need
could break any sail

a rain of tears, a mist of disdain
now loosen the cords
which error twisted to run secure

two stars dear that led me lie hidden
with art and reason sunk
so the port I seek slips further away

Hearts Rebound

after Camões, 'Pus meus olhos...'

I put my eyes in a book
sewn thoughts
in leather
and left it by her window

but it was she
took those eyes
dazzled
with want

and made the words
break
even glass

a heart so strong
uncased
speaks back as ruddy splinters

Of Glass and Mud

after Rodrigues Lobo

Tagus, with what different cast
   we see and are seen—
troubled you are like me
where once we appeared calm

Your shift is tempest-driven
   robbing silver lines,
mine is a favour withdrawn
and a sentence carried far

Now that we suffer both
   clarity coiling to dirt
I want to go on with you
scenting the fragrance ahead

Seasons turn but will I ever
look bright in this valley again

A Rose

after Góngora

Born yesterday you will die tomorrow
    a fleeting spell however framed
though gone soon you will frolic more
    fresh in the naught that waits

if your vain beauty impresses
    it must—as you'll see—fade
since ruddy leaves hide a promise
    to wither and fall

when a gardener's hand seizes you
    strong to make the cut
a harsher breath will try your luck

still, don't leave, some tyrant
    may prolong your being
guarded in a bed that leads to death

Labyrinth

after Mary Wroth

Far underground, where shall I go?
Tunnels open on each side but I miss the way:
if I turn to the right love wraps me in fire,
if I step ahead ice holds me stiff,
maybe the left is best but suspicion lurks
and as for crawling back, shame blocks resolve—
a cross of opportunity bars any faint
and stopping still is harder, even to regret.
So let me take the right or the left path,
move forward, back or stay put:
without clearance I must bear this doubt
and work a track to read what attaches.
Oh, what would ease my troubled sense most
is to leave all and take the thread of love.

Turn of Carriage

after Elizabeth Wilmot

Nothing feeds this fire
more than scorn and disdain
I to swell your desire
used kindness, in vain
you just spurned a slave
that juicily enthused
hope not then the power to save
which cursedly you used

you grow constant through what bores
caught in some snare of consequence

though you still have my heart
slight and rigor I must feign
there remains no other art
your love fond fugitive to gain

Wild and Smooth

after Baudelaire

Knowing my bent, she keeps her jewels on
when stripped, a tinkling bracelet and necklace
which mark the zone we ply, amber-black
in the dance-hold of our eyes' embrace.

Stretched languid in the pillows
she smiles at the swell of things unsaid
between knowing selves, a creature lit on dusk
whose purple lips rise from tawny skin.

Arms and hips in a curve shiny with oil
lead to her thighs' spices, that tempting cave
where quiet is half-deferred for impossible
shifts—minute to hour through a seam of need.

The lamp dies and the fire whispers to stone
as she, infused, bears their blood-glow proud.

Matter Enclosed

after Baudelaire

My skull is a pyramid sunk into rock and clay
with pipes like colonnades stretching
through caverns and muddy corridors

here a diamond waits behind plague-green walls—
a flash of liquid metal whose apex dips
and thrusts up as a mirror

this hemisphere is the glare of a streetlamp
in a vent, sliced words that half recall
the tapping of heels and rumble of traffic

bodies bloodless hide in the eye that would sing
in bony silence, though there's a rose
and a lock of hair folded in one stack of receipts

it's a granite cell and a vast park, empty
even with stuff irrevocable

Street Crossing

after Baudelaire

A roar of traffic shuts off sense
but through the pall
a woman passes with a white hand
lifting and swaying her scalloped hem

graceful, statuesque in stride
she has me drink her look, possessed
as the sky that would spawn a hurricane
drawn to die in frenzy

a lightning flash—then darkness
a fugitive glance to suddenly remake
(paired before eternity)

elsewhere, too late, never perhaps
neither knowing where the other goes—
you who I might have loved, you who knew

Probe

after Pessoa

How many masks do we wear and undermasks
on the soul's features, and if in play or strain
the soul itself removes what finely tasks
some essence, how can it know the face is plain?
The true mask knows no inside to what's out
for it sees each state with co-masked eyes
so consciousness must always hover in doubt
as habit gives tissue to the front that dies.
Like a child frighted by its mirrored gazes
cold solid against emerging self
our souls foist otherness on worn phases
and get a whole world on a forgetful shelf.
And when a thought would question the strip
involved, it's born with a blip in feeling to grip.

Racked Grace

after Montale

You know: I must leave you again
and cannot—like a well-aimed shot
every act every cry shakes me,
even the salt breeze
that floods the quays
and makes the springtime
harbour murk

this ship-mast forest laid with iron
in the evening dust

a long drone comes from space
screeching like a fingernail on glass

I look for the lost sign
the only pledge I had from you
          and hell is certain

Motet

after Montale

Shears, don't slice that face
alone in my draining memory,
don't make her heedful gaze
an endless mist
of half-things that press
to elude

a chill falls . . . the blade
slashes silver
and the wounded acacia
shakes off
the cicada husk
a tymbal song
shut
in first November mud

Night Passage

after Pierre Reverdy

We are two
on the line where all meander
a word between
two mouths which don't see
a sound of steps

a light body slides to another
the door trembles
a hand goes by
one would like to open

the ray stands up, clear
and it's the fire separates us
in the shadow where your profile strays
a minute without breath—
yours in passing has burned me

Safety Catch

after Pierre Reverdy

I don't look for more in zero or continue the rave
don't blank out what I face

release a blade of light on this rebel breast
impossibly so, a cobble bloodied

I only lie with one eye, a flap that opens
on forbidden hopes
a wilder recoil from a deep gorge
muffled at the bend of night

and then time and then the lamp
a step that misses with no going back
in the street's upward sweep
to tomorrow
from my heart to the world's limit
the stifling thickness of a wall

Heart-throb

after Paul Eluard

■■■■■■■■■■■■■■■■■■■■■■
■ She is standing on my lids ■■■
■■ her hair in mine ■■■■■■■■■
■■■ with the shape of my hand ■
■■■■ the colour of my eye ■■■■
■■■■■ engulfed in shade ■■■■■
■■■■■ like a stone ■■■■■■■■■
■■■■■■ against sky ■■■■■■■■

■■■■■■ Eyes always open ■■■■
■■■■■ she'll not let me sleep■■
■■■■ her dreams at noon ■■■
■■■■ make suns vanish ■■■■■■
■■■ has me laugh cry■■■■■■■
■■ and laugh ■■■■■■■■■■■■■
■ when I've nothing to say■■■■
■■■■■■■■■■■■■■■■■■■■■■

Scream

after Joyce Mansour

The vices of men are my domain
their wounds my sweet cakes—
may my breasts provoke you to rage
and my hair strangle your pole

Let me have you the way I prefer, fish
in your soul to find what slips

Into the red velvet of your throat
into the blackness of your stomach
I have entered
into the red satin of your ears
into the dark corridor of your eyes
I have entered
and the earth spins and sings
and my head unscrews

On the Job

Making it in this fold all kinds of
stuff comes through—
the nurse in a uniform wrapping a finger
her face pressed to the glass as a train passes
hand on thigh in the theatre balcony—
moments you don't summon
to gear things up
that B-movie throb in a pocket mirror
directing the pen to read a channel
not a life as such whether morse-terse
or full with berries and sky
I'd say the picture flips as all the pronouns
carry this act (Ovid sure or Sappho)
don't think this won't get tonguely close

Rig

Any ripe engine
will do it
to trace and kiss
of the great north wind
only to start again
in need blown about
finds an eye in a mole
a head lands happy
yet our bridge of arms
is nothing bolted
stronger in frailty
ah you whisper, ah
will hold as the moon's
present-absent

any quick wit
give me your hand
blocking gusts
in this fourth line
with roughened force
when thought borne deep
there on your breast
as if it's the end to all
with squeezy curve
that's how the spirit flows
than some fix for good
the glitter of this locket
voice on the page
in pressing to pass

Actualities

Jackson Mac Low turns Edward Estlin Cummings

somewhere i have never dead bracket
moved to unclose would it avail
a skew line to shimmer
without worship in marsh light
as even a nail joins skin on a beat
elfin when fenceless willing speaks
all in silence a lip mazing nill-we-plus
gambol O stir in red g-g-g-uess
AUMMM so slowly wholly it jiggles
any furnished stop a painter would try
through blue veins of alphabet
that habit this sheet the earth ivy
or bird's eye dashing the cabinot jacket
for rain fingers to play a spring just come

Twisted Circle

1994-1999

I

Pastoral

Snake paths you feel for and it's
cellophane-wrapped, the glory
kept precise as a rose
commanded crop and root
by a thin red wall.

Merry before the rim they go on
to pepper whatever's driven
so the scene is nothing wanted
in a costume series.

Thankful for a job and a partner
you'll not dispute the closing time.

Shots away, barely noticed
dreams are cultivated
on a little bone-meal.

Craxton's Premise

The dreamer sits, head tilted
into upthrust hand. It might be the lost
province, leaves an idea swaying out
to buttress the moon over hills.

Who said it was here, an entire word
done by machine hammers
or corded by émigré limbs?

You take the load, years on.
Sword-boughs twist in a theme
with ten variations. An oboe
broods a space for sparky relief.

Use or be used—the marks to make
it mean, by reticulations of light
in land re-nerved, times over against the bar.

In Melville's Track

for Eric Mottram at 70

A Jack is in the stars, spangled
in reels out of a toy-box: may must
ride it through, cinders blowing back
on the collar, a three-mile grade
to sing with a spiker's echo
jump-a, rattle and roll, from a cold iron bunk
or a labyrinth of filing cabinets.

Hunter at sea, a cluster striding
in stark December, shines
a red shoulder—a blue-white foot.

A civil heart won't drive meanness away:
the civic calls for a lightning mix,
a fit at full-finger speed. Word-warm
readies the cut of the point above.

South or Below

after Goethe

Do you know the land where lemon trees bloom,
oranges glow in dark foliage
and breeze blows soft from a blue sky?

Do you know that house? Pillared tall
with rooms shining bright
and marble figures who stare with pity.

Do you know the mountain and its cloud-trail
where the mule lumbers through mist
and a cliff drops sheer by a racing stream?

The dragon's brood in a cave,
myrtle and laurel above—
states of a line or stanza deferred.

Do you know it, the place, the path
where we should go?

Fragor

Inside Okeanos that pounds the spreading earth
a sea drawn from old pages
where monsters stalk
opens in heat
a casserole
changing colour

as Levante and Sirocco fight

thick seaweed and ridges

a rocket flare
at the pegged edge
of an ox-hide

Wax giants and a hooded penitent
treading the course of stars locked up
go into midnight, poised to melt or slyly escape

Sunprint

Red earth behind a curve of coast
that's a piece of heaven
come down. Across the plain
contenders file in a shadow
acoustic: thud of elephant feet,
distant horn, whistle of cannon shot.

A garden before pines and rocky heights,
each defile cherished. Part-morisco
heads carry pitchers by the dry rambla.
Wind-swayed olives, almonds
in terrace strips
tap veins of silver, cunningly
laid. Days pass slow
behind salt-white walls.

Capricho Oscuro

Black cloak dream of blood red cloud
morisco veins in glass
reach to conquer
and convert
torn back
as joke of a book forbidden

blissed landing
from Algiers dungeon
serviendo la causa
to white carpet
under green crest

fiesta, ointment to galls
then a fever steeple

pipes
drums
a chirping echo
to the plat of crackers
and pound
of Micalet bell

chant
before
jewelled
cup

might *pícaros*
in a clean square
translate
this rough
journey

Strata

As if to devise the key to make all sure:
mosque and temple, gothic
with a cross laid out. One flesh
walks from an iron gate
between thinned relics. Diana's dart
could be a leaf or blade, now
where that cruel smile makes a join
of pulses. Unbelievers stare
as knights in a far country, facing
a serpent that could be them.
Stations of gold or obsidian, blood rays
in candle smoke: the code drawn
against itself projects a flaming heart
will turn in tears a block ahead.

La Seo, Valencia

Cup of Dreams

Still and yet turning
to the sky's incline

a basin of light
in the court

        each gazer's
        thought-ray

            fixing
            to disperse

                shape
                and colour

            a glass face
            rendered

        through
        stone

La Boatella

Live without sleep, the cats hiss
down a narrow alley. Stray notes
from a café make glass clink over sawdust
as a couple lean back, pressed
against a car. All space belongs,
pavement, road, grass, in the clutch
and breath of night. Characters single
cross ruts of tribe and creed.

A can clatters. Eyes peep from a grille
searching for bodies. After the rain
where it pays to lie still and flat
saints with blackened hands and faces
hang from the vault like bats. Which side
did this, you ask, to the whisper let things be.

Saint Variations

after Gertrude Stein

Cubes come out of this country, a garden
in and outside the wall, a house built before
you can remember. They can remain Latin
if met and separated. Teresa, Ignatius—
how many are halving? A higher voice
in two against the heavier tone, blue
with silver gloves, wonders whether to follow
bits of halo that differ from anointed now.
Might white let settle the spirit led, surely it's
not to want him dead. Those features
are eastern wed in rivulets and blossom
but an iron sword calls time. Face and face
about, a writer makes it be third, to do
her whole in a decade where everything cracks.

Leapfrog

Away from inquisition, boys vault
careless down a slope. The bell tower
behind a tree and a line of washing
can't call them to explain. Nor will
the fluffy cloud over blue
dampen their sport, springing
through a loop: up in a pyramid
hands to back, so the figure
has brief-reign, and then a head split
on hard ground. Faults make you brave
as the bullring shows, a glow
historic at the far edge. Some logic's
left out and better—*laran larito*—
when a shoeless child is a lord.

Infringe

Loungers sprawl, leaning like propped fish
with arrested sight. Others bob as puppets
making a point with a spoon or napkin.
Coffee, obviously, is an event, spooling time
into date on date. All arcs at the table,
tap tap to sort what happened. They re-fight
the peninsular and a river crossing in winter,
when August brings a cargo of gold.

Talk is their fore-bright book,
its granular raspy characters marking
some dog division
in the proudest soul. One traitorous trot
jerks the love-tie and only tarriance
can bring biters back to the starting plot.

Blood and Sand

A cylinder glazed with faces, the roar and lull
of what is sought: steps of a dance
to reach your spirit-twin. He is spangled
in a suit of light, sequins framing
a thousand rays in the stomach. He is black
with massive neck and eyes on fire—
snorts and paces in dust. Each contained
to go over and beyond. He plays it
with a flick of red, invoking the charge
of horns. He is held in passes
bewildered, aiming the spike that'll prove
who is better. A dash at brocade,
a turn, *to-ro*, *to-ro*, a drive between bone
till one falls heavy—a heap of meat.

II

Zone Apart

Aside from gilt and damask . . . midnight bells
and sawdust on the floor

a clear vista
stretching
before, behind

just a white dazzle
on a plain of water and earth

a sail or a funnel,
mulberry and pomegranate

oil on our bodies the only daub
with northern cloth
shed

Round these spread limbs
the air invites a suspended ethic

Mesclado

In the Bar Nautilus when we asked who
blew up the bridge, it was always
the others. Half-smiling you wanted to pinpoint
the offender but the waiter was diverted—
gracias a dios. And should a crawling black line
reassert itself? There are black grapes
on the balcony, loquat clusters in the garden
and there's no need to enfreak the sitting square.

After this I wanted more than ever
the wreath of your sex, almost the mark
I no longer knew. You'd say exaggeration, all
right, *taraba* in false descent, but the time away
has notches to embrace. Ever a lioness
you want me to roam—the dying sun disputes.

Double Exposure

The castle on the hill is a locket gleaming
gold in the late sun—red-pitted stone
over a swathe of pine and oak.
A sentry yawns, leaning from half-burnt planks
on the watchtower. Maybe in a cleft of rock
a scimitar lies, not with the rude edge
you assume. A kestrel hangs in the air, silent
before dinner, as we mount steps beneath cactus.
Through rusty bars and creaking hinges
the sign of a kiss is given, not recent graffiti
but a long-played chronicle. She places herself
in front, says here's a hand in a black glove
to draw promises, if the troubadour
shapes his tongue to dig something different.

Clutch of Stories

Against the white wall of the villa
her arched form at dusk invites a different
hold. Seven years since we touched first
and still there are scenes to invent. She drops
her earrings in the bowl, runs fingers
through her hair and reaches as if to pluck
a lemon from the tree outside. She feeds
my want with a tropic murmur, hips rising
with a sandal kicked off. In those lips
there's the glint of a hundred plays written
and acted, where we squeeze to evolve
in the sea's skin, drawing out its purple close.
Now with parts surfilled we lie as one
with Rodrigo sketches and ribs of moonlight.

Tagless

Ardent looker
niling the plain—
never say dye but tint
eves any stain.

Grafted roller
avid to speak
ventures a line
in matter foreign
nabbed or unspied.

Just another joke in the kitty
always there but breaks
newfound.

Still Saraband

i.m. Jan Lubelski,
Costa Blanca, 1.9.95

I
She on the shore, dipped already,
reads, in aura removed
from the churning sound-house
as her man and their sculptor friend
go again to test and relish
that jade liquid frontier. A brood
of forgiven argument lingers,
four-bar phrases throb as the wind
sighs into sand, gravely arching
to exact requital. Another loop
forms on water and cries
two solo in strained performance
fear with welter and chafe
she cannot heed such muster.

II
Gravelly billows drive
blue-green tiers, majestic
in wake of storm, a drift
local with heave of stranger gods
to lure in late fierce sun
a keen floater or two
kicking weed under froth
plucked weightless away.

What it keeps on saying
the flood we can't decipher,
carved restless, ridge to trough
trough to ridge, in limbo,
is—*land-locked and tideless*
the mythic laugh will strike.

Salt Steeps

A trench in the floor which should not be, sand
scooped when the tide is out, truckload after truckload
to feed some road or estate—which turns oblique
the current at swell and pitch. Reason unseen
this back-pull brakes any stroke, or rather the reach
that would be made. You move in a frame, drifting
sideways and out, an actor imperfect for the scene beyond.

Days of blue on blue, glory to a duller palate,
linger Sorollan in a robber's caprice. Hard to think
how the picture lies, if the same is done over
again, but pleasure sorts with a stir of forces, eager
to wash and fix. Borne in a rheumy caress,
lulled by the buoying quire, we cross a line
where breath goes still, our oldest summons.

Spell

A film runs back and the trick is done,
Chaplin diving into a briefcase or catching a brick
in the crook of his leg. How you relished those gags,
the prison uniform instead of clothes a swimmer left
by the lake. A kick in the eye for what's assumed,
decoding a leader's speech. You had a tag
for any state, into the swill of error. Now *mala crux*
you've swallowed the text—a beached whale,
ivory white with a bloated stomach. Your watch
goes still, rim shining, and those snared syllables,
Hannibal to Byron, slip from the choppy flat
to the grove beyond. A ring on one finger
suggests an orange you plucked. Would you wag
that digit to reverse our rank in a witches' broil?

Fire and Water

You are become the force that pulls
to free a body

sought as one to avoid it comes
weighted to make light,
at full metre
has you turn and twist

clanging Sophocles in the brain
over pitted floor

***

there's nothing after, you said
embalmed with a stranger's smile

all goes in a glassy flame—
bone and flesh to ashes
the readiest mode for return
on another plane

still, in a heavy nought
some aura bides

Totem

An orange plastic tea-strainer, the one thing
the villa lacked and which we bought
in a market, now supplants silver.

Black liquid sits
beneath gauze,
leaves apart
their work done.

Each cup poured with a dash of milk
brings the chooser back, tells
the mix of green and brown
as oil in the base a current translates.

Adrift: eyes, lips, fingers
crave to fuse, and this rite
is a bind to gulp and go.

Rip

When you did not see or hear
you prised him away, as if the same syllable
could not exist either side of another—
a triangle given. But my shouts were drowned
by the wind, you read your words
in a shell, while a spirit was snagged
like one precursor in a tangle of rigging.

Waves flood the house, it's all coming down
while we tread our usual steps. A figure,
his or mine, passes the window twice.
I grope along the ground for sense
as you shift objects. A cold embrace tries
to restore the moon boat, with oars floating
by hazy shore. How different is peopled alone.

Stalled Moment

Why one should return and the other not
makes it the same scene over and over,
though both were delivered—one alive.

Responsible to who, as arms grip
like an iron ring.

A stark mouth spews words
with the subject gone. Was there ever
a solid in this flood
driven across a raked level?

The room smells of rank seaweed
while belongings cluster.

She, a crimson slash, would tilt things
against relation, and I (once here)
feel the press of leagues in a sunken bottle.

Dark Premise

She comes to the fore through shadows,
we know but forget as a story
twists—one dissolving through another.
His eye fixes on her blouse in the café
with a half-drained bottle to rouse talk.
Gently he tosses the towel round her hair
over a single lamp.

A camera has gone through the pane
to find what's in parenthesis.
Our own script, precious, slips into copy
for a second lead.
As the phone pleads a wrong number
beside the bed
it spells how we started to meet.

Love Gristle

And now the pulse is visited back,
what made her eager to entwine
in secret rooms, woodland
or furniture that's home.
She's half-left these red sheets,
fondles 'devoted' as a record
careless on the floor
which anyone could break.
Why won't you treat me as him
I imagine, the preferred stranger
who makes you late.
Don't conflate the man
I drew you from, safe in stock
with one who ventures to bite elsewhere.

Montage

What was then is always present
even if we cross our steps
oblique, mourning eyes beside
quickening hand. She pens my part
when silence squeezes
lips, a throb
that devils any probing member.

Can't live with you, without you,
can't shake your glow
from the passage I delve or keen.
Some other paces this dip in terrain—
spumes the lie of unhappening
grace. Those pivot hips that matched
my jive ... speak all I'd ever write.

Imprint

The pillow is you, a feathered mound
left to provoke like flaming june.
Do I have the language, even, to address
that state, back-phrased as the light swivels.
A quatrain strains uphill—it's perfume on a pin
looking to affix, when the clue that does
is just the element within. More than this
there's nothing ... don't make a bogus man
with shivers. Shouldn't we, couldn't we
have all this—ocean to devotion? Say your name
I nearly understand, count to ten
then down again in a bid to shift the frame.
What is the song, who's on piano you whisper
from another chamber, sharing a thrill at least.

Bipolar

Truth is a pitched roof with the moon
sliding above, a circle intersected by a bar
that doesn't hold—as pine rots
and slate falls in a fretted stretch
from bonding, you'd see it through
slowed time, the blaze or buffet or soak
which turns every colour and shape.

Truth is a fixed star with solid earth
below. Its silver endures in running out
of sight. A boss won't dull this polish
prized right to the rim. Spikes are just
a vapour blinking from a disc that's set
to sing. Tell me, aren't we right by heart
and fingertip, given light in the room.

Testament

If it comes down to it, with unlikes sparking
there's everything we saw between the shutters
or felt in a sprung pocket, from Blue Angel
to Kill Me Again, I mean each textile part
broke to combine, your fierce [   ]
under wondering eyes as the bad made it good.
If I did warp you wove our [   ] to the end
in a savage triangle, drawing the heart headlong
[   ]
[   ]
You live on in your stuff—a barefoot sea-girl,
finger between those open lips. Now the swerve
seems to cancel with red crayon I'm not
the gazer but still record, afloat in thick deeps.

Reversibility

Back for the night you give me the works,
an old dispute with window light
and then in unstale quarters
the spice for what's played together

squeeze of thighs to pull deep,
guide and receiver in trembling runs
over mind forgotten, salt
to the nave between wails of joy

So they're spread diagonal
skin to sheet
as if jack and queen never had
a different story,
she the speller and he the spiller
now exhaustive make a true goodbye

Limbo Line

A platform deserted, with wooden benches
and curved white tiles. 'Minadoors', the only phrase
a survivor has, wanting to connect. Thought I'd find
a hot voice in black lace, something foreign
to talk the day through. Maybe she hides her score
in a trench coat as champagne is fetched
and flames sway like feathers, all reverse footage
in thick blue smoke. Should either choose to leave
there's something worse round the bend.
Arches slip past, walls dripping. Bolts go clunk-thud
while a hat lies silent at the foot of a ladder.
Would anyone notice—a poet is automatically
a missing person. Fingernails claw the ceiling
that holds up tier upon tier of books laid in a ring.

Poet's Sinews

He strums his guitar, tracing a tune
she'd want before, the curl
of each little phrase

a spell passed down
that held even deer and birds
or rather made them stir.

Could be a viper's bite took her away,
I don't know, it's an old pretext.

Then, worth the toil, a scramble
down jagged steps, with faces to please
and against any hope
their stern permit not to look back

leaves the glint of a broken string
in exhausted air, a body torn apart.

Loquela

To see her lucid in flesh or thought
not a shard in the skull

and feel behind a blue dress
and Egyptian necklace

            that voice
        say honest
no one's the same to anyone else

maybe the parts we drew
        are a phantom parade

            the blade I prized
        is a has-been

whose lulls of silence
        break only
            for the rushing fit

Familiar

Flimsy sheet, if you even get there,
can sense be made of something dumb?
Strokes and loops pretend to link
soul to matter, maybe a tune, a hand held.
Bluebells on a bank, neck overhung.

What life awaits—shredded in a bin,
screwed to a ball, stuffed in a drawer?
Or propped on the mantelpiece.

If you are handled, kept a while,
note how she looks, with a frown, a kiss,
a skip to another place. Who comes
to the door like a ghost of bliss.

Not to spy but simply to be
a part that figures, there beyond any press.

Scaraboid

You put out the words—a stack, a scatter
to get through night, stretching what's before
in an effort to close. Tread slowly
a bridge of dread that climbs into mist
till something in the staring world catches.
From a bed of mulch your legs, wings
turn waste to richer fabric, as broken light
on a shield gives the means to roll.

Your tenured rival will jeer it's the same
on same, a snap inflated to a feature
with druggy ah-mees. Sure, some gloss
lingers as a shell around hefted blocks
but this measure plays from the mind's heart.
Who bites to laugh gets bitten tomorrow.

Sea Grammar

In the haze comes a floater
foam-necked
with wings spread

    crying high
    with slipback

            just/at least/maybe

     the judder
     of specks

            on a rib vault

threads wagging from the floor,
tangled faces

bequeath a cordage
     on the sodden green—
only mast-lights among the stars

The Cure

You think you fell through a trapdoor
or was it the jaws of a dragon

some mirror tangle
to smash another's hold

it's easier to learn
than forget

face it, she made you poor
and the rhetoric should be spent

go to a different country—
savour silence

weed can counter weed

as the rust of an arrow
can heal the hurt it caused

so, for gods sake, stand up or give up

Respire

And can it be cleansed, even in a deviant line?
He climbs from cellar to kitchen, where
water is a burned body or a dampened flame.
Those words, caught in snatches, could never
be silence, the notes are etched in every unit,
sink, cooker and cupboard. Her corner
is a broad arcade where kissed unkind the urge
to finish gets further away. That earring in his
mouth like an opal lozenge carries the taste
of desire, from liquefaction back to a solid.
This door is the sappy trunk of a tree, this wall
the clay from a pit, we'll not contest
their shift through counter-states. So it's agreed
there's a time to clasp and a time to get clear.

III

Quartet

A leap between two half-steps, echo
to echo, finding by withhold
a build of fragments. A quirky dance
flung back in here we go round
throating a drone. Gut-sear beneath
nothing heard—just a vibe down a pencil
in the mouth—coaxes a song
that weaves respite
slow in a god's time remove
I am not you I am the self naked
as form itself. A little swagger of a march
pretending to amuse but quaked
at heart. Nervous heave to bring home
what's before, fast cries to lead in silence.

Eye Play

Candles and a jewelled bowl—
some red liquid to spin the brain

    no help for it, you must
    must try again

big green leaves around the room,
two holes in the wall

    faces stuck together
    like a pancake

who would be in the market
again

    at least a little turn
    squeaking saxophones

long after midnight, one murmurs
Come back to mine

Circumfuse

I just want to sleep with you, she said
(meaning sleep)

I need a monk beside the bed to watch over me
but then there's the sex

a body to play
neck and rose-hole

is this ever One

a demon in green leaves
mindful at heart

dawn is a portrait with hardly open eyes
the flaring show you'd not hasten

a poem across four lines

her take of him as robbery grace
the glide to trust on a crimson sheet, trickles far

East of Absolute

for G.E., dark
in the filmic brief

Just any taste it is
not, I swear
when you rib my nights
recorded before
as if this were less,
some desperate habit.

No, it's the juice
of a burst pomegranate
and if I more haggardly
rise against the myth
that seems, give me
the swell, the allowance
to give, not most by words
but somethingly so—by default.

Exile Dawn

Talk me to sleep
with tales
on your purple leather sofa
in Belsize Park.

The judge won't tell
who the daughter is
and under the rose
your cat I swear smiles.

It's a long way back
to Clare and Kerry
but blink and the reels are here.

Slow a concertina eddies
from Valencia crepe, jigs up
by bodrán to Apples in Winter.

Idiophone

A single note
struck and held

a bracelet of waves
quiring white from blue

as eye on the sea-line, does it
look back

                                        words only
are only words

                    you push outside

the waste   to carve

a presence   lies

true   a swim

inborne   for
steading

Thriller

Over the road and up the hill
we step into night

a door
to alpine green, frosted mirrors

and then into further night

a long chamber
with velvet seats

tipping to engage
a drawn square

She makes the thing unfold
that takes her into a tango

a weightless body for leaps and kicks

without a home
surely I touched yours

Portage

I think of blue silk over a wrecked chancel
and have to go back.

To breast the same waves you can't
when different courses flow,
plumed cobalt or haggard grey.

A whelked curve breaks
into a net of foam

salt is all men's tears
and a seed in yawning void.

What is allowed where words come
in fragments?

Off land the wader treads over slime—
better dry one voice says
yet moist things exhale a pilot soul.

Prado Gaze

Before a garden deep-vented to the sky
two play out their dream.
Hand on the organ keys, he looks back
into her secret space. Bare on a drape,
she fondles a dog, distracted. Not always:
detection says her first profile tied with his,
nothing allegoric or if so in lighter spirit.

Velvet folds import a join of sense,
the taut skein that pitches to a cry, let go.
Same-strange figures mark the green beyond:
a faun spouting water, aligned with music's sword,
a stag with head inclined and a strolling couple.
What just happened or will happen next
we wonder, inside apart through gallery beams.

Vihuela

As an emerald set in a work of gold, so is
song with a jug of wine. Words in red cipher
wind over plucked notes, felt
at the edge by one bound on a galiot-shell.

Age lines in varnish bring forgotten gods
to the hall. Waves circle one column
and tip the ceiling to a bed, with ingots scattered
in slime. This we believe—to a death chord.

Ah, Venus you are a dark girl by an olive tree
testing the man who looks. Stay here
with another air, sounded from the heart
of a waist-cut vessel.

All possessions pass, strings and curved wood
but something carries, a phrase or two through dust.

The Clowns

Mannequin or human, cut at the waist
or simply by view. Their costume,
gold discs and braiding on blue
and the same on cream,
marks identity in duplicate. One presses
an accordion, the other holds a trumpet.
The fuller, smooth face has stiff hair
winged and rearing, the tighter face
has a hat fitted proud. They come back
in the mirror behind, a poised magnet
with a hollow suit, stuck in the grave
for wanting to laugh. Will this act
go phrasal—will it, will they lift
a bottle at the edge, a dipped trumpet.

Stop the Beginning

A lid is firmly down, he cannot let himself
feel, but the virgin with gold ringlets
and snowy breasts steps out of the picture,
minutes before muffled in a gown. She's here
in the cell and there in the garden, turning
a rose between her fingers. They must be
equal sharers and not blink if a vulture
appears in the nave. A vow broken is another
made, though in a room hung with black
some rope, wedges and a mallet will serve
to persuade your blood to gush. Questions
come quiet in a mist but two centuries on
if the door is open, leave. There may be
a crowd outside ready to applaud such nerve.

Language Cabinet

Shells and sugar-papers on the floor,
head of a bull against gaudy tiles.

        Come from a stone bench
        the men liven
        over glasses
        or little cups.

A dancer's body weaves—
notes held from the south
with word-stones
rubbed.

                We with paler skin
                a counter-masque

        trace the line of wrinkled gold
        open all night.

Tagus

Tawny-yellow spirit, gold veined in song
with grains tried from a sierra knot
to run west for the sea with arms
splayed. A voice splashing
to encircle and flow on, by white poplar,
willow and tamarisk. Haughtily rough
it waits for a woman to descend
from a lonely court, one who by magic
changes the old course. Under arches
she lifts an oar to begin crossing—her dress
his boat with scarf unfurled. A breeze
repeats her face in ripples, the faint smile
and deep-set eyes. In this bed the narrative
reconstructs, hair waving in water.

View and Plan

It's not down in any map, true places never are,
the teller could say, as one book
sits on another with matter ready to ignite.
The river girdles a green hill, or several
that hold crowded behind a wall
a fortress, monastery, houses. Language converts
in steep, windy lanes but the patron healer's base
is thrust forward, a glistening model
on a cloud, while an earthen jug pours profuse
under swirling angels and a she that gives.
You push the question back, what is
a place assumed, just a thing in the retina
that obtains at every step—stuff caught
on an inner coat yet feeling where's relation.

Floating Nous

What's recovered in a bundle of papers:
our story told in another tongue
touted as real. When Virgil's a magician
talking to a brass head you need to finger
the text removed, if it takes nine years
or more. And then there's the crystal lens
with crossed blades on the field, not exactly
tropes for the ordinary. She sat in a marble chair
at midnight, left this coat and disappeared
in smoke. Well, such deeds are an invitation
to joke. Just stand at the rim and look down—
elsewhere the scholars are mute statues
but here Avicenna rubs shoulders with Boethius
far and close, like organ notes in a chapter cell.

Gothic

You tell me in the Greek's studio
you saw the snow on fire.

Candia gave him brushes
but this rock, heavy with relics
in a kind of grief, gave a better pull
by two zones of trial.

He stares direct behind a hand,
the stiff ruff joining states, but even
in prayer coils of a snake betray
purpose and a flashing vein
makes the sky come down.

The line once started will never return
to itself. Here it's stretched diagonal
in a gash, dissolving any case assumed.

Voice Geometric

You think you're outside
but you're there in the folds,
the pearl tint of an olive tree
against a blue wall, wine tracing
a river-bed. How surrounded
is a hand or eye with translation at stake.

Things are pitched metallic,
a gleaming blade from an archway,
a crucifix in a cabinet, a bed
painted with gold leaf. You walk
this maze of pounded granite
in a fever to know, an actor
from a fossil theatre
seeking today's word.

Posada

A photo from a great keyhole
in the Arch of Blood shows a dangling lantern
by windows garnished with flowers
and guarded with bars.

Nothing remains where the sappers came up—
courtyard, kitchen, balconied rooms
are a frolic novel squashed.

Buñuel is a priest wrapped in bed-sheets
who will never revisit. A humorist
here is a bad fellow.

In agreeable retreat honey is too good
for a donkey's mouth.
Banishing why with the table laid
giblets slither in a snow-heap of rice.

Exemplary Tales

Dr Glass, who's eaten a Toledan quince,
says a poem in a pocket of greasy papers
has all the arts in one, but voicing a sonnet
can't get his listeners to attend. Repeating it
makes no difference. He steps out of straw
and, at a grave Latin pace, claims to have
better answers—yet now can't bear a crowd.

On a hot summer's night a roisterer
sees the woman he must take. Wiped out
she hardly knows what's forcibly worked
but, come to sense, notes all features
of his room. Seven years forward
with a child in hand, she has the means
to exact blood, which fiction turns to accord.

To Want or be Made

after María de Zayas

A small candle of green wax
at the top of her headdress,
a gilded pin stuck through the heart

will summon a night-gown walking
to give all desired

but what she remembers is just
a dream

They say she feigns enchantment
and should be locked
in the hollow of a fireplace
behind rubble and plaster

you may prise that red leaf

but our heart-story is a black forest
where no one can find a path

The Weight

Which of these do you prefer? You must choose
between two grapes, two bread rolls
or two snowflakes. There's always something
that makes one of them better. Even chick-peas
on a plate. His massive desk and bookshelves
are the pain of centuries, with slippers
to fetch. She puts her arms round the pillar,
stoops over marble lips, reaches for the clapper
in a great bell. It is his head, severed. Now,
which alley prevails? The cloister is draped
with hedge-mustard and ivy. Passion should be free,
no chains, no signatures, no benedictions. She
opens her gown on the balcony, drawing his gaze.
The wind whines through telegraph wires.

Emerald Tablet

The viper in the gorge turns green, then blue
twisting to advance. From a rugged bed
its liquid skin gazes back with marks
of each figure that passes. Not quite
the branches in light or clouds overhead
but shapes freed into dream, an ooze
thick and clear to draw what's
elusive. The scales call, languorous notes
inviting a plunge to grasp a nugget.
Coin, bottle, jewel might answer desire
but one person's god is another's con-man
driven to heal by poison. Better the chill
of close walls, apart from a street furnace.
No, the burnished demon compels, open to try.

Archpirate

In a hole below you may speak
to the devil, learn a thousand tricks:
to look into a sword as a zodiac
and recite the psalter backwards,
return a lost object from the shoulder
of a sheep, stare into a basin
and restore losses, make monks eat
when they should fast (or fart
in the cloister), serve pastries
of tow, pitch and wax at the feast,
have a surly carter gallop in reverse
and a greedy host waive payment,
impersonate the figure which no one
can get to know—and be cast to die at sea.

Memory Palace

Gridiron

        of corridors, courtyards

                mark of a man

        who roasted

or shout of faith contained

Grey bunker

        lined with white

where a world   is ruled

from two sheets of paper

Dome over pinewood desert

        a stretching compass

                teeth, ankle bone

        in granite

stare to stop time

Green Fort

A pine cone shoots

a crystal plume

that falls through a grille

to the basement below

where jasmine, lemon, orange

hide

from the harsh north wind

To keep limits

and go over

todo o nada

under a brassy sun

this garden

is a kiss severed

continues to press

Folio Version

Close that door, shut out the war. In these pictures
you see yourself hanging or holding hands.
Two virgins invite you to supper, as the crags call,
and you drink from a skull-chalice. There is no
stay in this arabesque, the snakes writhe
by a gibbet like pieces of rope and wheels.
The track up here is one corridor after another,
they say wanting to embrace. Nothing can equal
our sunny clime, but life can be cased in a helmet
to draw confession. What formula will explain
jasmine breath to a storm roar? A sort of aversion,
a tiff and then release. Sniffing, snuffing the candle
an end comes closer, but riding along the shelf
it starts again: a woman beckons, a body swings.

Affinities

Paella at midnight on a long trestle table
under crystal faces point-cut
in a black curtain.

Light breeze after sun, dropped
like a stone. Half Africa
held in guitar notes.

This is the only province, she says
in a curl of smoke, each word
throatily pressed.

Water drips from a pipe, feeding
the lantanas, by default.

Scent of oak and berries in a glass
ruddy for the spill of anecdote.

A spirit nocturno calls from a tree beyond.

Field Repeat

If I could find that flame in the heart
with roses and castanets
I'd stay where the dancer turns
a startled lion. To recover the same
thread—steps, words so foreign
and close, spinning in a fierce embrace.
She like one before leaves a graze
on the back that speaks
of wrapped hours. Would you last
unglamoured beyond these sore lids, coaxing
the swish of hair to brush? A sea without
known waves, these are my hours.
Fore-sheet and mizzen cast
the future as bells take you home.

IV

Default Reel

Bold without tie, he moves through a sea
of faces, the teenage rite done over
in dim light. Words pour as wine from the half
that engage while tact or fear clams
those at the edge in an awkward stare. One self
pokes through the skin of another, am I
an actor singing or the monk who so records.

From that chain of chatter to a pool of space
        dancers spring and spin. Held
at remove the heart's still beating, ready
        to put the dit in the dit-dit-da
and feel it almost perfect. Smile into eyes
        by a rhythm dazzle—the soft
guarantee of a world you'd not believe solid.

Seed

Maybe the marble hall was underground
and lemons with the imprint of teeth

    maybe the mute statues bear witness
    not shut off from feeling

maybe the sharp rock-face and water-burst
were the heaving of Tartarus

    maybe the green laurel that inspires
    was part of a bargain with Death.

Now the broken column rises
with drums re-formed. She, a sleeping guest
will wake in silk, bearing shoots
from the other side. Only a sure touch
can set the calendar forward
but you can write without knowing what.

Eye Switch

You're either Mr Theatre or Mr Worry
she said and I never know which
is coming

when Spanish
can turn
to languish

through sea-tongued fire

round an apron
of land

Allow this, never to force
what belongs

as the chain on your breast
holds a stone

black in default

Autonomic Stitch

Here on rug
as Cambridge field

the script is open
which is to   which is to
let   all we've drawn   apart

in lifetime halves
here   and   there

come
point
to curve

feather touch
firmer hug
glaze-glance

belong in poetic fit

Root-Room

We play for keeps when a hard-set note's
torn

moment to moment

apart from overlonging

that hill in cloud

we wanted

to reach

Sunset crosses

this sash

the candle

is a column of breath

You can wait for something
without
knowing what   it is

Centre Aside

Love in her person shines, not
the flaunt of here am I

a care for what's
given back

or simply there

in a walking mind

fingers to button

open

nipple in mouth

speaks trust

a swollen surface
belying any idol

the creased clinch

of a line lately found

Forest Traces

A safe harbour   her curving quay

for herrings boxed

under the main head

zig-zag paths through pine

up between straggly stems

spice columns

leaning for breath

maybe to meet

a red deer   a stuggy pony

at the reach

of wind-shorn turf

furze   springy   rushy land

you dip and climb

each day   a fresh plot

The Wanting Story

Too many words

go lean

into space

a remote shield

with iron studs

which is not

a believe

to number

like this pot

red

on the window ledge

bears

a stem with leaves

bud and flower

Heart Reach

As if grass were our pillow we walk
in dream

hair touching
where others' tears
have fallen

the scent about of pine
our pledge in joining tenses

your scrawl in the lovable west
a track to match my imprint

bird flutters

through dawn

in deepest night

we are finding the nest we've forged
snug in a twined cup

House of Song

A poem is a flickering solid—
thought, experience left in manoeuvre
through to shape. You say devices
suck, making a stiff of the motive finger
when currents wind otherwise
beneath above or cross-diagonal.
I don't know, the go chirp of what's
never told, a name on the glass
or a boat's black dot against dawn
have their part to shrug off
contrivance. The thing is to open doors
where the paper would blank out
demons at cool remove, so not in show
the tongue finds links from other space

And in the Frame

Are attic pots with lithe Nike suspended in air
and horses grazing. From a trap door
some smoke, the curve of late revels, is voicing
what passes with rhyme. An oak twists
into a staircase, its rivelled surface ready to carry
coal and eggs. Along the corridor
grey with dust a clock laughs at the sloping jetty
where a steamship hovers. It will sail
across floorboards as something claws a chair.
Beyond jealousies a woman looks back
at the mind looks out at her. Could be the screech
of brakes or shriek of a tawny owl, fairly
knocks any plan. We start in a swerve, extended
by habit: to write crooked in straight lines

Hill Tongue

On Grabbist the wind would never say zur
as it moves up-along

        a spirit careless that leads like a finger-post

over ling and gorse
through spindly silver birch

            a path feeling like trespass
            in a purple head

notation foredrawn   or   dotted fresh

        the giant leans in his chair and waves
        down a deep slope

watch on walker in river dip   braced knee
under tree-wolf   how shall   its reach attain

hump to airworld   where a warbler shortlifts
scratchy rattles   batter-bright   and we paired will sing

Vortex Rerun

More then the rock amyddys ye raging seas
The constant heart no danger dreaddys nor fearys

Rising from water fury that might be
a womb of leather or fur, the triton
captain tries to punch out Peace, who,
calm in a black-rimmed quarter-segment,
strokes his arm, as in the moment beside
(or behind) a ship founders, mainmast broken
over crew leaping to boats. The face of a corpse
ruffed in surf floats between rock and skiff,
pointing a way perhaps to land. Brother
of a hero, he'll inherit for a spell
after the sweating takes that voyager
come through wrack and confinement
to a glorious rest drawn in the sky
or surrender worse than a storm.

H[ans] E[worth], *Sir John Luttrell (1550/91)*
Courtauld Institute/Dunster Castle

Danse Macabre
(Recension)

1997

1

Summoned from work, day on night, who's the dancer
conning? A touch on the arm or shoulder: 'We were once
what you are. What we are you shall be.' Big with oversight
this swagman keeps no calendar. A face out of the funnies
grins in triplicate at a life extended like Zisca's drum.
Got to meet him in that day, return his smile. A bug-word,
a letter edged in black. Scanning to order the lay of the case
a font of knowledge strikes from one mind to another,
a green lion grasping the means. Who would follow
down this tunnel or linger ahead? The frisket bites,
the carriage runs in to the second mark. Your word
is thinged in the winding-sheet, pressed as linen or olives
where a challinge comes up for diallinge. Rip the calico
with scenes transposed: what more dangerous than a poet.

2

It all comes tumbling. To find the core I went by steerage
with sail spooning before the wind. To save the hull
we let all the rigging be damned. Phrases culled
above the pitch, out of tune and off the hinges float
as the lyre, the head, of Orpheus. A chart of a chart signals
rawly the ore in the dirt, the skull in a velvet bag.

Love is being locked up. With a wedge, a quoin. Held
space of the page. Against the drift, a hell-pledge.
Receiving an impression with force she lies in the coffin
that will be him, rhymed as halves of a perfect heart.
Love is being loosed. With a stick to reap. Kiss-tight
in the galley, to be ink-moist and through into the hanging,
heaven-fold and dispersal. Our wits stretched out,
we are mischief for the taking, wisdom prized in play.

3

That joker got lucky beyond the rafters of his body
tilting an engine against *decora* and the grave sentence
to frisk by tinted panes. But talk to him tomorrow
and the massive frame, the wooden screw and straight bar
are broken monuments. Those eyes, those hairs, those hands
are an echo coarsed in the courser's record.

The fourth in the background has no double, he's died
enough times already or he's the innocent here, pounding
his bauble for Minerva—a scape that may not alter sense.
Two deaths lean in tune with the uniforms, left-handed
to take a batch out. The other, whose sprigs of hair
and fleshier mask could signal the absent female, bonds
with the leaning pressman. Death's finger points
each function but won't stay long either side of the post.

Days of '49 outtakes

1997-1999

Gol-durned Curtain

Which way in by a battered sign to prise out
stuff we knew, a puckered face that cries.

Today's Friday, come back tomorrow
or Monday.

Can you speak two spokes
down a square hole and a propped,
twisty tunnel.

It won't light up like a jewellery shop.

You'll hear Tommy Knockers before you blast
and might want to bolt.

The nugget's behind a hundred tremors
that make the world we brave.

Spriggans will chant a spell as your tab
swallowed, to get the beginning to colour.

Travelling Eye

The past is clear enough but it's
a flat sheet. In a yard of familiar names
is there any 'there' there

        one farmhouse at the end
        of a long bumpy track

                a fox's path through a line of oaks
                before the yelping of hounds

Give me any word on the perplexed surface
where a hole looks through to nowhere

        we thought we were killing the enemy
        but we were also killing ourselves

                a land in fits and splinters

its stuff just a retinal catch

or the ply thrown

Feedback Stages

Can you take me back
up the slide—maybe the words
in some shut-off tower

speak us
a line in circles,
everything that's been
or ever will

found hab-nab
with syllables swallowed and a deal of hiss

* * *

What if this wire
translates to an iron rose

can you keep the slack, so things run
kiltered scally—a delvish chain
all laid out and coming

Man from Yesterday

Do you ever get premonitions? Yes,
I get that sort of feeling about my income tax.
There's something about the orient
that calls—the light, the smells, the music.

Bank clerks don't understand this emigration
of souls. I rather welcome the thought of inheriting
a new shell. That tune bothers me. How is it possible
to play something I never heard before?
Music is a series of vibrations, every note
breaking into space—a span over ages.

Funny sort of chap, though, always reading.
It's unwholesome, prefers to be indoors.
Poison is sometimes harder to identify
than its symptoms. Will he sort or be sorted?

Imitation of Life

The Ratio Club might not approve,
dining whip-smart with no professors,
but the tabloids have it: Elmer and Elsie
know what to avoid and where to go,
heading straight or crab-wise
back to the hutch. They could be kettles
or toasters, built in a backroom lab
from old alarm clocks and gas meters.
A sign says 'Please don't feed'
as they follow the light. It's how
we're wired, shell on a tractor to plot
things first—a tortoise with brain meccano
fixed by a rebel. Slow, this forecasts
a will controlled can slip every control.

Tutor's Tale

after Michael Innes

Suppose we were Roundheads besieged in a castle:
would it be tyranny to insist on a proper share?
How slow and painful is every step to a better state
when a man in Whitehall tells the railway
how many slices of bread and scrape it may give us
and just how thick to cut the railway slab.

PLUTONIUM BLONDE shows us in the dark
dispersing trails of light—a bang hiding a gunshot.

The expert cracks atoms much as we crack nuts
but he can still be hit by a cream jug.

You're in the corridor of an express train
its outer side cut away. Miss Liberty stares blank
and sightless—or it's a clock face with no hands.

Perhaps the brain's more vital than the paper plan.

Back Row Watch

When you're trying to fit back in
and grasp a solid rail
the relief is to tap what's filled
with moving. Buffalo and a wagon,
tiny specks on a yellow sea, come closer
then a spread of sage in cracked rock.
Out for a high stake with smoke ahead
they have to decide who's boss. An arrow
or shotgun will settle it—in light
that never was. Hand me a can of coffee
so I'll find that ranch with good grass
and water. Ah yes, for eyes turned west
there's a join, but busted out
you can't ever fence what you are.

The Walking Hills

A poker game to a blues song in a backroom
in a border town

like I was sayin'
there was five wagons in the train
with five million dollars of gold

headed straight into them hills
and never came out

forty years I've looked for a strike
up and down every range like a cat

and now the young'un finds a wheel,
that skinny kind from a hundred years' back

We leave here tonight and dig
where the dunes lean and crawl

a punch (ran out of words), a sandstorm to open or close

Aftermath

They did their duty and then clammed up
but some things you can't keep secret—
they travel in the air. A dead man isn't
as much trouble as a wounded man,
people cling to a stranger when nothing
can last. It's hard to raise some colour
though stuff flashes like gold in the ground
with all the grit when you sweat yourself dizzy.
It's a sort of crime puzzle where one can't be
dragged away. Tinned milk and spam before
you start, the diet's whatever you can grab.
Ex-service, who isn't, out of jerks, jars and jingles.
I'm a used-up man, a perfect used-up man
and if ever I get home again I'll stay there if I can.

Home Ground

It's hard to go back to the house
pinioned, reading backwards
against the pressure
of the door

you see peace in the mirror,
a summer of sun-bleached grass
where a lawnmower calls
or a pot on the stove

it might be a bobbin at the latch
with a different feel

who's to do what now the line is moved,
she with a lever-phrase and he treading blood
to conceive a likeness that'll refigure
features fought for—in a spill to grow free

Judgment

after Marghanita Laski

There are a lot of gaps, empty windows
beneath battlements where a star might shine.
Could the boy lost be a version of you
found eager for trains and swirly marbles
in a wrecked town? What if he doesn't have
shining hair, high cheek-bones and deep blue eyes—
marks of your beloved. He might, they say,
have a poet's mind or fingertips.
Don't you wonder with every stranger
what they did when pressed? I've had four years
to stop feeling anything save in print.
Did I give? Was I ever capable of giving?
We should do good where it is near,
where we can see the end of it.

Four Star Puzzle

Follow me quietly
at night—
high heels on a wet pavement

She's come to interfere

A dame from a pulp magazine
won't help

Maybe this dummy will show who grips

Here in the office to tease—
a blank face in a chair

Restless reader of just her title

Off-angle it's the Judge
climbing a catwalk of pipes
that burst like rain

A true crime rookie she gets her man

Peekskill Blues

When war is done the enemy doesn't vanish,
he's somewhere over there waiting
or he's here under a hood with the same words
for all that's wrong if you sing and dance.

Hammer out danger, hammer out warning,
we'll not get lost in the wilderness—
a river and hollow down country roads
where some say 'us' isn't wanted.

They'll burn a man in effigy, set chairs alight,
thinking to clean what's black or red
with clubs and rocks to turn speech back
in a line that makes a programme.

Shards of glass after jeers and taunts
are just like history passed—a spiking crystal.

MoMA's Façade

A statue voice pivots
from an upper chamber

comes crisp on the notes twirling
out of bone hair mouth a screen still

for wave-break fingers a rocking-horse
in the drawing-room

rides a maroon-marine road through pearl-ropes
to the sand's brassy band

so pigtail steps demand
another little drink at hell's bar

I am the poet surfaces—a bird in a gold cloak
with almond eyes in alabaster

her Plantagenet mask, a little outside life
fêted in a jazz grid

Phantom Mannequin

And there appeared in the square
a woman with a head of roses
crimson over a white satin gown
and black silk stockings

she faces the gallery beside a lion, calm
as pigeons perch on her net-glove wrists

the column notes a gaping hemline
and peep-toe shoes

your sometime object
walks a day mark in a painter's night box
fluent in French for Roussel
and ready to turn pronouns round

will open glittering handcuffs
in the whoroscopic record

The Mantic Stain

she feels
her form
as rubbed
in the grain
of the door

knots in silken
skin
with flashing
aura

that walks

a brain-
breast-
vulva
eye

Hold Shot

There
in the net
a fisherman
sleeps golden
his almond face
at point conjoined
with a shell necklace

not squashed flat on
a city floor, spiky
arms writhing
or a monkey
dead— but
a groved
olive

Station Legs

The barrow stirs—
green spoke
bones

at the bottom
of a peep-show box

        turn

with a ballad pulse

      don't tell me
      there's no such house

to re-walk perhaps
a stranger

the gouged field

scenting another
presence

Wonder Notch

Kin gassed   studio gutted

now this

swirl of slopes

risked alone

a trackway

through cedars

weather-struck

as a quarrel

between tenant and lord

Your eye climbs to the peak

over indigo turf

an Austin cell

or poet's tower

fuses glowworm, nightingale   in freer air

Reverse Lordship

Under the hood of ash and sycamore it must go
to meet that way more used. The nettles say
we're forgotten, the blue sloes don't know us
and this by a stile we fought to keep. A mile or so's
gone missing without barbed wire or an iron fence,
it's just a habit lapsed. On the map the line
stands out but someone's needs will leave it a waste
fitting a house or field to the empire
as a robin got drops from the cross. Now let loose
we'll stride anywhere with boots proved
but in the gathering—site on site like Domesday
through the looking-glass—simply the words
may trip, they do and don't mean what you think
with the kick of a rescue skull by a rag-castle.

Portreath

Feet construct the face of the land, a sudden here
in scored rock—hill over basin and jetty
clambered to slip down. Waves press a cleave of bone
like black hair on Spanish skin. Along the beach
a fitter or rigger walks to find, driftwood wedges
spotted with glass and Perspex, so a Bostik draft
can render the harbour's tongue and elbow.
In a painted state the copper lies flat, grey against
tufts of brown, the redbrick house is just
a sloping square, the daymark's absorbed in granite.
Before the seeing takes flight this is as good
a try of space, to slightly answer whatever distorts
it might be a cube but it's got the ground inside
labour spent, mining ore to the ships go out a ghost.

Long Count

The thing is to have a plan, as you'd do
with trees springing

to keep stock on track,
to wear clothes without holes

        takes nerve to restrain and push

a vesting day for a better life

maybe the little man in Whitehall knows more
than people do themselves

        but they want what they see over there
        without bolts in the brain

a leader has to get others to work, he's a chairman
if you like

        we'll have a bonfire of controls

and we'll nudge the project forward

Domain of Arnheim

An arched window with green curtains,
the lower pane broken

jagged pieces
on the floor and sill

rocks and sky
a shard-strewn glare

peaked like an eagle

The perfect scene is shattered
or lingers out of reach

its cold printed within

the land you try
an eye forces back

blood wall against the crevasse
a bar over any heaven detected today

Gaugeless

There are moments when it doesn't seem so far
like a pencil found under a cushion

                                                            the voice
of who got to be me, lobbed
before that skeleton tree by the road

*****

                                    It was yesterday and still
we're here, doing it again

                    not god forbid through a pre-set game
with props slipping into fable

or in that domain where *emporially*
a creator has to express
the matter

but now a pronoun turns to thistledown
I don't know, you can't, you'll never, I'll go on

Shadow Real

Television is anti-social, the picture's
too small, it's the world's prize time-waster,
it's not an art, it's just a passing vogue
like jazz or the magic lantern

but who can forget seeing Mr Chamberlain
step out of the plane at Heston
with that scrap of paper, or Len Hutton
scoring a triple ton at the Oval
or Bois Roussel flashing past the leader
like a black streak to win the Derby

it's fallible—an actor may fluff or faint,
but we're locked in a cosy compact
with what emerges from the turned heart
of a piece of wood

Bluebell Girls

No champagne and no touching, feet away
from waxed moustaches—base rule for the British team
in a Champs Elisées club. You must be five foot eight
with an oval face and be able to kick your spirit
into the noise and heat. A flash of magnesium
to the sax honk, seven nights a week on the platform
with corners of red and gold. You're never naked
if you're wearing make-up. The Eiffel Tower
has cross garters of black ribbon but that can be left
to the French. Here there's a swish of ostrich feathers
and headdresses bobbing to the beat in a temple
or circus. From ballet (too tall) and a Soho audition
virtue has come to this—you're out in the middle
rehearsed to a T and the show is the only star.

Bed Fare

after J.B. Priestley

But why detective stories, why not
some calf-bound memoir
or travelogue
to lead a grumbler through coils of time
after the day's knocks and greyer business

To turn on the right side and open
bottle green covers with the whiff of caramel

You might not know where to fix the guilt
but you sense there'll be a solution
ethical as Socrates

Those final meetings in the library,
those little dinners in Soho with six pounds
worth of claret, to astonish
into recognition a mind that won't switch off

Man on the Eiffel Tower

You must distort colour, play around with it, make it work for you, intentionally throw it off balance. . . . There are times when nature is dull; change it.

Stanley Cortez

Not the obvious freak, a knife-grinder whose thick lenses
bounce light back

shoes can be borrowed but not fingerprints

says the ruminant pipe and overcoat
gulping a cup of coffee in Montparnasse
to see beyond each sentence

a career on the line and a life—
it has to be someone else

and a head that pulls off the perfect crime
craves admiration

it plays with the head that probes his own
so who's following who?

a scramble up lattice girders, giddy Seine below—
iron eyes say 'jump' but the demi-god walks down

Time Unpast

I must tell how I see this table, this chair,
this box holding my bottle of ink. I must not
put in strangeness where there is none.
You force the truth when you're always looking
for something. I must never [   ]
but note all that happens. I'm already
too far from yesterday: the children were playing
ducks and drakes and like them I wanted
to throw a stone into the sea. It can't be thought
unless it presses now. My pipe is daubed
with gold varnish, look and it's just a streak
on a piece of wood. Jazz is playing, there's no tune,
only a myriad of jolts, but some of these days
when we just *are* the point may come to shape.

Smart Division

She's glamour and hard graft, punching
the keys to keep house with children—
grammar right—and knocking back wine in heels
at the Mandrake or the French.

A princess for whom seven mattresses
cannot conceal a pea
will turn on her side and bear thc day
to a lover.

He who enshrines her is gone
but she takes another, marking with a crescent
the edge of pages.

The Mill's a muddy castle with prophecies
hidden in the library. She dances through smoke
to put the verb back in.

Yardarm

6 pm at the door, then through the Public Bar
to the Saloon, always to the left end
for service, rooted in a cluster of regulars
soaking beer and scotch, never letting it show.
Teddy-bear coat, silver-topped cane,
cigarette-holder, he builds on an old anecdote,
dialogue cut finer with dark mirror lenses.
Popping a green bomb will keep him up
to write. Simenon in an English harbour—perhaps
but why not *Night & the City* or *The Midnight Bell*?
A hardboiled man holds his nerve in a game
of Spoof, like when the other half bursts in
to say she's leaving, next month's pay gone
and rooms switched. 'Really?' as the heart dies.

Characters

One has an art magazine in hand, always due
in a few weeks—he's signed up
the poet laureate and the dean of St Paul's.
Another is the King of Abyssinia, reclining
in a white robe with his lady friend, a typist
in the Ministry of Food. Talk of mountains, coffee
or a palace crisis. The yellow waistcoat fellow
has a monk's belly, can be tapped for a loan.
The doctor who performs abortions also plays guitar.
Another is producing a film—he's got several
of the assembled under contract but they've
never seen a clapper board. Fixed as the Pole Star
a writer does his editing at the bar—anything
to escape the average in strokes of what is near.

Poet's Dream

Half-way down or half-way up—you wish
yourself out of its cleft, a black pit
in the hanging woods with church set
over mauve or smoke-grey water. A site unlikely
for prayer though worth striving as the sea
grinds rock and a vixen wails
at the barred window. What purchase
for meditation when you climb a distance
through oak saplings and ferns near the stream
one week in spate. A farm above could offer
shelter, stag's antlers nailed to its cart-shed.
Where exactly to plot that visit, turning
with two grains swallowed—the land read
as a book, bright orange puddles to honey dew
(withdrawn).

Maid of the Mist

Who are we then, a little heroic with the help
of other tribes. One angle says it's the core upright
with accent clipped and a certain skin—stamp
with deprecation. Up in the air you ride hands off,
look down as crop-marks in a dry summer
draw feast or memorial spots … they are not
tree-root holes, surely. East of the Windrush
churned with plough and warring tread
that dark oval might be a ditch. If the white speck
is an eight-foot stone you'll catch something more
in time. Dew will dunk a bank of daisies
after lovers have it hot, and Saxon strips will lie
on a Celtic field cut by hedges. Now with no clue
my Moth goes bang into dust-whirls.

Other Tears

after Luis Cernuda

Machines turn to ruins the tower they built
leaving a flight of stairs to nowhere—
mirrors rimmed with gold, a measured smile
over china pieces which survivors steal

pearl vehicles smeared with soot
line a desert where wandering bodies
take fruit from distant colonies
and force order through screaming traffic

now the dreamer who hid, a tenant chained
to a hole of vice, stares at the silent sky
from which vultures poured death
on figures beneath, a mass condemned
to pay back whatever's visited
that still searches blind for the blueprint to live

Blitzweed

Net curtains, rain—repeat
Sunday

a black pit
under twice-fired brick

is a broken jigsaw

where blown seeds
yield lunatic spikes and flowers

purple, pink

with insect hum

it's not the wireless, that's

a redstart perched on a stack

whistling sweet hisses
arced to a crunch

so thickens   a chancy strike

Histo-strip

Shiny helmets and black bodies dash
through fire—might by a flick be the ray field
on another page. But it's our world
with the sky serrated and you can linger
on a frame. A line slightly interrupted
is a hail of bullets. The normal suspects face
across, crawling from drains or dropping
from the air. We didn't finish them in 1918
and they rose again in '39, so you need
to be reminded. An adventure sells, vhroom!
Only picked men can be used, like yourself—
may I say rather reckless—fellows who stick
at nothing. Three-two-one-zero, without
an option you strike: Go to sleep, squarehead.

Engross

Fitness and Sun becomes *The Sun* and then (ahead)
Sun Adventure Weekly. If you look at a close-up
through field glasses it's turned into *Lion*
with a mortar barrel set into the cliff. Here it's Huns
at a radar station but it could be slant-eyed weevils
or ice-cream wallahs. The antenna rotates and stops
when a hero cuts the wire. Later they'll jam
this frequency. Sorting the thing is easier now
on cockled paper and if someone tilts their tongue
a message climbs into space. On the alert
is there a communist code planted into his flash?
Maybe it's a jokester's beat but with the right links
a fine name can get decayed or stupid. Oh, no,
by golly—a mirror, I'm firing at my own reflection.

Armchair Reading

He speaks with a craggy face
beside a roaring fire. You the viewer
he might have met in a pub
craving contact

How was it, yes—the camera moves in
and twists—that little resort with casinos
ripe for a stunt. Sky writing, letters
a mile long and audible

REPENT REPENT
they think the voice of heaven
to reform a town

The tricksters crashed
driving back but who'd believe this story
laughs the Lunatic director

Scanners Live in Vain

A writer moves through whole throngs of self
watching, watched and doing. Out in space
you can still every sense with a chestbox
willing blood away from pain and fear:
cities burnt below, borders fixed in peace-pretence,
menschenjaggers hunting any Other.
Safety is talk with a tablet and nail, evading babble
on the view-tapes. To drink in the sound of air
you cranch wire round your head
but a dash of food and music isn't the up-and-out.
Only prod-persuasion to eliminate
will make a cylinder sleeper defy the mass
as nerve returns. Not to follow an order
breaking the rule is a way for the first to go back.

A Sort of Traitors

after Nigel Balchin

It's all so hole-in-the-corner but science isn't
something that stops at the Channel.
A man who thinks of the world with flies
sucking his forearm would want this news
out of a steel cabinet—the blueprint
to block typhoid or the plague.
Think it over, though, there are people about
who don't love us much. Let's split a bottle,
what Winston used to call an easement.
Why do the tables in Soho always rock?
Showing it to anybody could turn a defence
into attack. We've got to live with people
but how big's the group at issue? 'Unmuzzled'
is an equation with different values for x.

Humdrum Master

A country living for preference, the young man asks
as the Bishop traces a Norman arch on the margin
of a letter. He gets it, a rambling barrack whose gates
hang drunkenly on hinges—marshes and sea
with a bank of shingle between. Muffled thuds, a screech
make his body bob on the waves, while his cousin,
Minister of Iron and Steel, is impatient to inherit.
Party politics have always seemed a nursery game
but he will scoop the pool. Lorries pass in the night,
maybe for a lord who does his best to forget
he's the son of a patent medicine vendor. Poacher-shy
he draws his cut from stolen goods. Petrol's short
and it's hard to get even stale rolls with meat paste.
Privilege rips though the plotting stays unconnected.

Situational

after Josephine Tey

What colour is a lilac when you are not looking
at it—with shut eyes, five minutes after
or seven years away? The face of he who disappeared
is a child's drawing, the outline true with details
to fill. Did you sing, could you ride a bicycle,
which arm did you bowl with? That little horse
with mock pedigree, all the tests at breakfast
before a lawyer's gimletting eyes. If in a pucker
he didn't smash on the rocks he's almost
cut-to-measure, ready to slip into belonging.
But twinship forces a bind: when imposter
confronts killer, neither can tell without losing
the base they've got. If either is brought to justice
the family falls, and besides sisterly love wants more.

Field for Shadows

after Phyllis Paul

Once she had climbed into the boarded loft
and pushed up the stay of the skylight.
She could not see out but she imagined
one might see right over the town

now there's a dim light in the hall, a slight haze
as fog creeps in. She thinks
of unknown cupboards, the black slits
of half-open doors, a tap trickling

she sees a girl going upstairs, head bent
and half turned away, one hand on the wall.
Like the time she saw a deer's antlers,
maybe an imprint of those below

we're sick of blood-letting—but how
we miss it, with just the scent of roses around

China Spells

If the march arose from C which existed before D
which hung upon B following A
how does it happen that they all appear
in the same moment

a sword-dance through yellow grass and mud
a year in a hillside cave
a lion with a cloth cap anointed to wake

say the cauldron has rings of jade, it is filled only to the rim,
promises nothing that wouldn't act to further
though if it tips   pause and wait

a comrade in the field has sun-red cheeks
and coal-black hair   the eye always will shape
as matter glides   no, it's not a miracle to share land—
this mind-broth is as much outside as in me

Earth Abides

after George R. Stewart

The trouble you're expecting never happens,
it's always something that sneaks up
the other way. War, with cities blown to pieces
and irradiated zones, hasn't come, just a virus
like super-measles. A survivor can live
on canned stuff, find a mate and breed
while weeds or ants invade, but rust eats
the pipes and girders. The library is a museum
with piles of wood-pulp and lamp-black—
what use the skills of Rip van Winkle
when links of recognition pass? A tribe revived
will lose water and have to flee before fire,
though spear-shafts and lion-skins
could take the end back to slow beginning.

Era and Error

Remembering it the morning after was difficult—to remember what you'd done 30 years after... it's hilarious—and on camera ... There's one bit, Ringo's telling a story, and he says, 'At that point George had a sore throat.' The camera pans to George, George says, 'I thought it was Paul,' and the camera pans to me and I say, 'Well, I know it was John.' And I've worked it out since: If Ringo thought it was George, it wasn't Ringo; if George thought it was me, it wasn't George; I thought it was John, so it wasn't me. It must have been John, he was the only one left!

Paul McCartney (1994)

Before the staggered house of our restored selves
the moment comes with a clank or whirr
slowly like a hand-braked four-wheel wagon—
was Jean in London with Cliff at the Hamburg end,
dial glowing a soft amber, did Cleopatra's needle shine
in rose-red granite, could the tubular skirt give way
to the sheath that shows through hanging panels?
Memory doesn't deliver our choice but what it pleases.

And if we weren't there in the mirror-backed public
just peeping or piping from a crib at our moon trinket,
can we . . . into revolution leap that threshold
so bits swing together in script? If a lion could speak
we wouldn't be able to understand, though
once seen, jungle Bill could help with a pill or two.

from *Le Fanu's Ghost*

2001-2006

Liminal

Jasmine in the corridor,
a delicately gloved hand in an upper box,
somebody muffled by cloak and bonnet

she wants the man who always sat here
who spurned the love of some lesser donna
treading this stage in *The Country Girl*

she might have laughed
in the Farce of the Parrot
but she hanged herself from a door
in the Garrick's Head

now when the curtain rises
she's always here and she seldom appears,
a sort of shiver down a steep rake
which prompts the best in each player

Cenci Face

At the end of a long corridor
between velvet curtains
parted

        she speaks beyond
        any name assigned
        as subject

pity and believe
these violet eyes
these red lips
this slender throat

        a count's daughter
        so caught
        will not betray
        either grief or guilt

Stalking Grove

A hum inside
prick-eared leaves
and knotted boughs
glint of a watching lens
must be the wind
tosses and strains
that host of limbs
which now would walk
and clutch the window
a glare of ravens
on a sunken stone
its groining the link
with what's forgotten
a drum in tendrils cast off

Looker's Likeness

A hand grips the banister as he descends but wasn't there
when he looked behind. Is it the Glory come to rob
a life or a box of jewels, the light of a candle at its tips
white and cold? He knows nothing as he explores
the house, a door opens and a bar of music jangling
sticks over the chess-board floor. There are footprints
where nobody walks and the corridor looks modern
when a panther hisses—only a cat, if you're not a sucker

He dreams he's on a lake sculling to Snakes Island
which may mean seven aiks—you can't escape
the other part. As long as it's light perhaps the stain
won't emerge, but once the darkness begins to fall
something white comes out of the water, her clutch
to drag him down. Still, he bobs up from the deep to live

Peep into a Whiskey-Shop

for Ivan Pawle

The doctor said it might be dodgy on the banks
of the dodder you must get a dobblenotch
to deal with dollmanovers where a demonican
soul would itch and cry domnation
so give us half a pint of sweet Pea will walk us
straight in a stretch at Hollantide seeing
what the film discloses it's neither sin nor shame
to drawl like an old collegian whinding out
of reach . . . when you've taken your skinful
you're fresh as a shamrock with dhrums & fifes
lording love and glory and isn't that a blinking
star over a drary draphole—the dombkey hangs
by a brassy doorplace and for old Linn Dubh
who'd be a dogpoet leaking any tale at dawn

Short Takes

2005-2007

Busted Levee Blues

Tough luck, it's been coming—cronies
on the watch with eyes closed. Folk will always do
in a place that care forgets, pay no mind
when the walls and roof rattle, it's a freight train,
it's the bass of the band up the street.
Sucking, bubbling, gurgles—who gets left
when the bathtub fills. Windows pop,
the furniture goes, plucked like toys from a box.
I'm clinging to a branch that can strip flesh
while a dog and half of a house float by.
A plan awaiting study sounds like a screwdriver
in my ear, just throw us a line or a boat to row
through this reek and monster-mash.
Bad water, bad water, it rolls all over me.

Change My Luck Blues

And blue is red you tell me so
just before election, I wonder when
I wonder when, they'll take away the alphabet.
Some's sent off to die, some's dodging tax—
these I hear is natural facts, don't tell me
about the tonic. World is full of talking pistols
say you'll go down with a golden hug.
Play them a long time, play them Beethoven,
courtesy accidental. Leaning to the front
they sneak the backness back, powder
to make the 'fore day creep. Swiftfoot isn't
how needmore get you, Tambo and Bones
syncopate the vote paid out
then let it fade with pretended sloth.

Tight Time Blues

Mean things happening all around, it's tough
to find a place to be. The face at the top's invisible
shifting its name from deal to deal. La-la-lu
if you don't like it somebody will, paid elsewhere
through a little hole. Might be another country
with nothing to furnish or save—a fool or a mule
can do it—or might be the brother behind your desk
who smiles more for less. Eight hours in the morning,
eight in the afternoon, with crosses for a break
makes a soul turn inside and groan. Mooching's
in vain, they'll sling you out, I waked up on this—
a job is a means to rob, so take your bonus and toil
in the loop where one calls and a line comes back,
it'll tone the bell that hides till we get through at last.

Playing Policy Blues

With regard to the question now occurs
refer to the previous state (figures different
or the dress says so). Who drew the dome
didn't go for flickery logo but staked a gateway
some handsome ape might follow
even when disappointed his pager calls.
All teeth and ears trouble won't stick
as the rules change, exploded from nineties
to noughties. Er, y'know a domestic fellow
throws money tightly, pleasing key shooters
under blind trust. It's a double act
to offset carbon prints or tag a suspect
God-drawn. Don't think to move
on a lie, mother, hand on history's dial.

Policy: a daily lottery in which participants bet that certain numbers will be drawn from a lottery wheel. (Webster's Collegiate Dictionary)

Snatch It Back Blues

Cheers some hooted, the stony heart
to shake and brace a lolling dream
vented, against all seeming habit
of me-first you-win tenders. Cleaner hands
with a speck of decent dirt would steer
the fuggy wagon along what's given away
to get health stuff back. Cool ladyland
brings in a guitarist for street cred, sings
how to sort the squabbling crew, over here
and over there. Mission grants licence
to meddle, a faith chorus richly argues
and on the rebound cuts her own
with a nail or gag. Knowledge walkers
face a stunt a week warning: don't bite that.

Frankenstein Blues

They tell me there's a new way of being
spare parts made into a whole
can do your job with a jolt of electric

ooh-ooh, they say they've got the form—
compared to what

I hear someone's crunching numbers
to cut the middle stage, keep the feelgood up

ooh-ooh, boot and goose on the output scale—
compared to what

Don't push too far for a magic fix, it's made
as the maker this second birth
all room and soon with stars in a box

ooh-ooh, you know when the spirit takes—
compared to what

Sugarland Blues

like stormy monday
like midnight black
like a fire-bell ring
like funny money
like a freezing toe
like broken words
like wrath for pity

just try once more
just twist the view
just look just read
just climb a dream
just shuffle degree
just walk a pi-ana
just to quit this hole

Pig Latin Blues

Ome-cay ere-hay, ome-cay, ere-hay
et-lay, e-may, ell-tay, ou-yay
omething-say, at-hay, ou-yay, ought-ay
o-tay, ow-knay

E-way ook-lay in-yay e-thay irror-may
ith-way ick-thay ashed-lay eyes-way
ere's-thay ourage-cay ehind-bay
at-thay urvives-say
aco's-dray eeze-squay

Ive-gay us-way e-thay east-bay
ho-way ill-way ing-bray
orning-may oney-hay

Hat-way ummer-say an-cay ake-may
is-thay and-islay ee-say o-nay imit-lay

Between Tongues

2007-2010

Lines after Andrew Hill

The place inside, silence within speech
that's on the go

        a pulse of black notes
    refusing to settle

brain-finger a little monkish   the way you wouldn't

        brood into swing

guess underneath   and over

            so nobody's a prop

the stammer the cough   puts time   in a spiral

with stuff laid out   you's-me

about to be   the coil in the booth next door

glass open   (no what-of)   takes

        a pump of blood   vibe'n bass

into grace   hits and breaks

Beneath the Lid

Signals cross
on the flick of a knob

shortwave slots through marble

a voice in horsecloth
a voice in lavender
a voice in a bottle

jeans worn under a cape
that tear your status

a gold beak spits iron splinters
to a contra-canto

bang and skronk

on a fluttering bar

the red hand of chance

will someday at midnight   seize and deliver

Dance of Paroxysms

The wind won't sleep for a knight returning,
he's two riders on the skyline, one heading left
the other right

why don't you join the dance
with a crown of thyme and marjoram

you could have this gown
spun from moonlight

the sky is the sea swirling, he must get back
to the one who's waited

elf spirit don't take me into the trees
I can see the bough that breaks

one stark finger will mark you
as the ground lifts in pieces

the one who counts lies still, like he (in recognition)

Library

The giddy page swings, it is all
the cobbled streets and pitched roofs
you have walked, forty paces ahead
and twenty back, a stack of orange blocks
in a mesh of black and green

Our speaking place dips and rises
in a boundless frame, with railings
like cable-stays and corridors plaited
to reflect the fold of shelves and stairs

Here is a spine to decipher as squares slide
into lozenge or triangle—the thing isn't
wasn't or will be a single presence
in ruled air, as in the pile who can say
what'll best prove witness

Rego-lation

The child or is she a doll reaches for a candle
to get beyond, as a crone with beady eyes
holds fast her leg

        she says a sleepy girl won't get outside
        tiles that flicker, cobalt and white

what if a saint swallowed by a devil
should burst from his stomach

        a story in a land embroidered with waves
        can't close

now they dance while the fortress looms
changing partners

        he wields a cane
        that will score your dream

blood filling the sack to sometime go clear

Secret Lexicon

Night is a passage
blocked
with white fingers

a cellar with a tree
inverted

fever boils
icy
between floors

ribs shine
like beams
beneath coat and skin

Lips tumescent
she climbs
the spiral ribbon

Occultation

Why do I write ■■■ not even your name on the packet
withstands all proof ■■■■■ of the vessel in which
you sailed ■■■■ saw leave ■■■■■■ and in spite of all
I breathe ■■■■■■■ thanks for this despair ■■■■
better than the cold pleasure ■ your French mistresses
give you I could burn and tear ■■■■■ these tokens
you left in the room ■■■ I rarely leave ■ would suffer
still more than forget ■■■■■■■■■■■■ there's nothing
here to wipe desire ■■■ with a lighted candle a rosary
and ink-pot ■■■■■ ten thousand things in flashes
to say would I could send myself ■■■ in place of lines
when you write with repetition ■■ on paper half-filled
ought not to let you see how ■■■■■■ I insert myself
■■ in every act of yours ■■■■ an idol created for itself

Ship of Mirrors

after Mário Cesariny

The ship runs through a forest
shunned by its owner

no port will give her presence
with a cargo of rolling air

and a door in her silver mast

different captains stare
with the same jacket and cap

when a sailor revolts
he's a thousand mutineers

in the eyes of a fly

any climbing to scan the ocean
will just see stars in space

salt horizon swallowed, a fish
would swim where berries grow

Anti-Museum

for Graça Capinha and Maria Ilene Ramalho

An arm-bone reaches up
behind a glass panel

for verses
on a scarlet pillow

pulsing between surface and core

does each syllable
want
to touch

profanely in a chequered panel

its sister semblance
to get the way

tagging loose a domain
a new brood

as the moon held by a kite string

Santa Clara Moment

Where does (what) go? Bread
under her cape bulges, chaste in dark folds

        but it is just a bunch of roses
        to any who'd pry

as beggars reach up, beseech the floor above

        a roundel, a glass star
        by the *crânio* bell

* * *

January cannot curb their growth
not with a tongue of iron

        so rio Montego
        swills over button-stud cloister

when a better scent leaks
from one coffin

Who'd throw a stone at a rabbit?

Saudade

Her heron neck sliced for nothing
done wrong

            eyes that gaze,
            arms that entwine

Still the fountain pours—
proof to the last day

   against a father's disgust,
   do whatever you want

She's queen out of death, with robes
and crown

        each eye-hole a promise
        that others may kiss

her skeleton hand
young by this river's reach

Inside a Journey

Beckford, Southey and Byron came
and Coleridge saw its striding edge from a ship

    Dora Wordsworth rode the pine-green hills
    saying she'd wipe Childe Harold's sneer

this earth is a slide of bones
as the gushing water goes elsewhere

    birds alight on grey soil and sing
    a perplexed music

some space of wrinkled sun leaves a bloodway
to the quay mirrored black

    eucalyptus is paper but oak stolen
    will leave only mushrooms

it matters who wins in the cross-fold
but is it surrender to speak of war

Quake

Hoarse thunder below
waves hurtled
into trenches gaping
a slide of cracked marble
as books tipped from shelves
from a far dominion
for a cup dug between hills
will this earth never be quiet
a sailor searches ruins
twenty thousand houses
an act will bounce back
so here in italic ground
without reason
but nature does its thing

black stifling dust
high as a spire
all fire on the wind
wall, stairway, pillar
pink with gilded letters
sung as praise
miracle on lease
in lines of shock
buys a woman to forget
of six to seven storeys
the priests pretend
you can burn slowly
a gauntlet to hope
to level roof and beam

Lusiad Core

University of Lisbon Botanical Garden

Can a power that takes give back
when leaves and roots
got at the dreamed margin
live on behind this stone wall
in strange endurance

the traffic below hardly touches
a blood-oozing dragon tree

it could be a rainforest
tangled with columns and giant feathers

ferns, palms, fossil gymnosperms
spread without notice
on a slope pierced by slithers of light
where time inside time
all our names know your leap

Bailout

Trees bent over ruined fountains, mutilated heroes
in armour. Pyramids of rock-work guarded
by marble lions. An ample supply of jasmine
to inhale

Walked home by the light of the moon
rising behind Serra da Arrábida—its streaks
quivering across the vast river

A flight of steps,
a terrace against rough cliffs, a Latin inscription
under crinkled pediments. Quiet crevices
over water where words ripple from foliage

It is another century with cars chasing the dawn
and no trash in the graveyard. With a charter rigged
people must feed or pay their debts to the devil

from *Hariot Double*

2009-2016

Tonal

Plum talk is just the way we got it
out there. More Britt-ysh in pitch
than the clipped drawl that toggles
here. My bell is not the zipzap
thing, it comes like the moon
through a window, gold filigree
on the wall. I can say *hapstickle*
but that's toddy from another tree.
I knew this game before I saw it—
club-wise stride in silver tie
with red stripe. You can't be just
an equal. Beneath one pediment
I'd draw half the world, chops
outworking any catalogue of habit.

Parish Without

Scent of pine needles on dry soil,
better than a voyage to Egypt.

    Sticks cast out, speaking
    more laws than you know.

        Belt of trees against wind and rain,
        air free to turn.

            Forget any clock-tread, breathe
            ahead and back

        leaf-oil to blood current
        in a burdened chest

    green finding red
    down wracked tubes

equal as a thing you might
invent, off beyond right here

Deccalian

A still box
with ribbed front

smooth steel arm
over sprung table

click, gentle buzz

pull to the right and start

drop, crackle,
furrow to centre

vertigo runes

then deft dial
through field

echoes
  of bird
in flight

Galvothermic

A line to plunge and spin

through memory pockets

the fight by the river, a Roman wall

a ring o'roses, a glass palace

proper muddle you're in

with yesterday's dragon at the bar

you shouldn't twist yourself

to make it

like this shove and crush in a wind-stream

***

now I strap-hang a radiant vein

could be shaping up

she sits on red-green diamonds interlocked

against brown woodwork

suede points tipping towards me

Thread

A drop down steep stairs and through a baize door
to where the action's penned—smoke
before a red bulb with shadows thrown oblique

a flame of faces across one table, a woman's throat
rising from the V of her dress as she sips
slowly—don't ever tell me I'm the new equipment

why the plural, you're most yourself in the other
you touch, beaky alto piercing the drapes
with partner-limbs finding time
and laying the breath field out, a ladder on air

forms parallel, which way, forward or back—
you trace it with your fingers, feather-delicate
for a firmer press, the groove around a wall or floor
that could free the tune bravely squeezed in black

Slip of Comet

When your drummer don't show, even Phil,
the gig is off, with no dough.
The chief gets shot.

You walk by iron palings, statues with blank eyeballs
where deep below the goods honk and whirr.

Seems you've finished a bout with the world.
The chart on the wall is faded, might be
your own features.

Five to one the signal isn't remembered.

Barber's boy, MJQ recruit, heaved palladic
to a void.

How to stick—is there any ligature, dust spotted
braid or catch, to guide a bounced body
back or down that Frith-set space.

Fourth Sign

The crab, a Say-nothing sort
must be somebody
sideways

chariot

carry 'ot

'eary 'ot

flesh to shell—fluid and hard

as from a crevice you flip
slowly the note

salt massage
in blue
folds

clasp what seems to go
wanting always another home

Tune as Weather

Uptown to Downalong

a spied variant
through toxins

the Sloop, the Castle
kiddle-e-wink

somewhere
the spliced cable
of self
will
quyt a fyll
(utterly fail)

and make
I won't say a saint
go *muzcok*

Pallatyne Knot

The ladye Dorothy at Essex house
for the river showe: fiery balls in the ayre,
floting castles. Then to White-hall
(against my lord's will, for Tongues
shall clatter). Her mother sayes
she must goe forth, gallant,
to the Banketting-house
this Valentines day.

As a parcell of these nuptialls
is to be performd that play or Maske, *The Tempest*
by Mr Shakespeare

wch shall fill a peece of greene cloth
and resound the *Companie.*

The Earle would have me watch.

Abyss

The finest tale can be broken at the butt of desire
as mischief works in furled light. You are near
that dreame-country when a storm is loosed
to tear the main-sheet to rags. No sailor can brace
the shippe as it staggers, a drunken man
climbing mountaines. All footing's lost in its pitch
as gusts pummel and heave—thunder and lightning
drive dolphins which friske to the utmost floor.
Now the maine mast snaps, its cable-roots
plucked from a firme base, as if heaven's pole
were shot. Only Venus can rescue a swilled hulk
stilling bitter breath with morning gold
to recover the pilot, who cries Land like one woken
from a droppe ten thousand fathom deep.

Jacobopolis

Mr Warner hath a letter from Mr Percie
who names theyr towne James-fort,
which is liked best because it comes neere
to Chemes-ford.

The river, that ebbes & flowes
a hundred and threescore miles,
where ships of great burthen may harbour
in safetie, is proclaimed the Kings River.

This Fort is built triangle wise,
having three Bulwarkes at every corner
like a halfe Moone.

There have died Captaine Gosnold, with others,
of Swellings, Flixes & Burning Fevers.

But howsoever, this Countrey is a fruitfull soile.

Jest Site

If you goe to Braynford a punke will have you to bed,
you shall pay as liberall as Caesar for Sacke & Sugar.
Yet you may mete who you will without after-buzze,
sit at Tables into night gaining muche from nought.

When the weather is rawish and cold a paire of Oares
will make foule speech as *Caron* hath taught them
but take you under tilt by swish or sway to anie reach
or miry bank while Westerne smelts like soules nibble.

Perchance the Meddowes of *Sion* will bid you practise
upon a Lute, which you must not breake in peces.
For this, with a sweete voyce or two over the rundle,
pluckes off baudie-traffike and puts all follie behinde.

Blood Vine

This, thought by some to be a bastard kinde,
is of all such the most goodly and stately,
having leaves like the greatest Willow or Ozier.
Its branches come out of the ground
in great numbers, growing to the height
of six foot, garnished with brave floures
consisting of foure leaves a piece
of an orient purple colour, having some threds
in the middle of a yellow colour. The cod is long
and full of downy matter, which flieth away
with the winde when the cod is opened.
I had these plants from a place in Yorkshire
called the Hooke. They do like ground
that is fire-burnt, which giveth force to rise.

Nightspell

South Hamtone

        to painim londe

a voyce

        drenched

by oare-thresh

        or shoke

in a cuppe

        of Misculyne

a lyon queld

        a lemman fonde

togedre

        lasse & more

this I thinke

        I saw

Motley

2010-2014

Sounding Cylinder

i.m. Kate McGarrigle

Take me, blue sea
toss and tear
a packet pounded
in hymnal rooms

even trash
you learn from it—
radio addiction
pooled out in the dazzle

we walk there we go down together
look the same and different
as a ribbon in catastrophe

smile bangles, moon-tongues
stillness to let
it glisten

Instructions for Angels

i.m. David Bedford

The stars are occupied, melody creeping in
and out   girls' voices in a sea
lifted by helium gas

                              what is this *sklitter*
read at the margin   with hair-like circles of fire

a pipe twirler swung around the head
or a moist thumb rubbing a guitar

                    one emerald field
with the slow brass rotation of a ghost
at silly Mid-on

                    let us choose the kind of light
when a dancer comes to pummel the keyboard

her moving sparks make an echo-shell
beamed for the time we're in

Crossborder Jube

for Geraldine Monk at 60

Gostwich fair, your glass is not to be matched
east of Blackburn and the riggin' that calls
ride the lingo off the beaten road
all coronal in slipstream as forbidden scent
lingers, gluegold to flaunt
daystar strain. What wordwake still
incites such fire, nine with twice seven
northerly? Who's touching anything like
escarp or gully, a true frame in false relation.*

Loosed a sprog from ID cards, tea rations
and utility chairs, you've fledged a style-speak
up/under Snake Pass, zedding a model
different—the '52 take with a pearly glide
Sheffield says it's the bird (and more) to follow.

---

* Byrd, *Ave verum cor*

Audit

so net
so neat
so natal
so native

so nitid
so nitrile
so nightie
so nightrid

so nat
so nether
so netflicks

so natty
so naughty
so netiquette

Glossolalia

after Artaud

mai kré pecto
coko roko rikera
klaver talekta triva
scaver kavina crolo
lober kiki kroledi
gonpar arak padera
lucro pendor villiken
rara dagwa caca

ankrolinkro
inokiramogro
dorakogo
onokamigo
aurakogro
orokogrago
aurologro
corodiralegro

crai bo doto
cras bada clita
scopro te goraquin
momar zingti quah
uma oova grilo
brimbulk driquant

ratara ratatara
hara totara
staraba katara
rara nadma
ortura konara
komako konaka

Devil's Drool

I always prefer sliding down the snakes
to climbing up the ladders—you can move
with a second skin of watered silk

        the table creaks and so does the ground
        if you listen, an eye opening
        among leaves

you get nothing for nothing, this house this land
the pools beneath claim payment

        nothing for nothing as a blow-up proves
        some goblet in a larger circle

I am not to be killed, I will twist red
in ribs on green

        give me one jerk of the wrist
        at a switchbox

Arsmetrik

The street sign buckles
and sags in the sun
while a viral stream
buries all sharpness of query

your face is a piece
of blackened wood
with orange peel for a mouth

there's decking board
where ivy twisted
up the old line fence

we swallow clock figures
thinking rice is arsenic
when key words block
any turn from the table

Waste Zone

It's not a marble thing in wooded hills
to find who'll go to the last ounce of blood
for an olive wreath. Even if the bodies
stay toned and willowy, it's steel tubes
over a concrete bowl in land that's soiled
by oil or hydrochloric acid and studded
with pylons, you might think a miracle
to clear—tanks, frames in a weed web
across the valley where thrushes, herons, bees
make life. A fruiting body rises purple
from scum or shattered brickwork
and a vole darts under a bowed bridge.
Can a smooth track, a push and a scream
fit us right on screen as a legacy bite.

Master of the Mainspring

You can print the ear whole from its cells
a thirty minute needle frenzy
buzzing round a dish
to bring up the shape with ink—
bio-ink that redraws the start, a solid ghost
growing glowing out of glass
flap and funnel to join with bone

You can scoop any message any habit
if you have the programme, dishfire or prism
with a smiley face for five eyes—
process, sniff and partner it
so there's no place to hide
the click or press is a beacon to tell
god's clone who's naked in the room

Bird Through the Wall

i.m. Alan Davie

How much more important   than this

just to be

a bird

the thing outside you

habits the head's

albedo

will swoop   climb   circle   green

on a cube

not the face you intend

but a three-leaved clover   or ace of clubs

hearing it   looking

click clash/bone clap

ting tang

mosaic

Land Spokes

1999-2019

Finder

The grasp of being above

stuffy heat
with noise

magnet in the beak or memory
of flecks and spots
to get the line right

a wood might be a blur but it's different
from a cornfield or range of hills

you won't founder
in chunks of wall

gleams green
through a cloud-slit

anchovy-sauce cliffs
by the wrinkled sea, blue almost to black

Kilmartin

Stone through turf, hollows covered to keep raiders off
but retrievable for bone-converse. Along the glen
eyes and fingers uninvited join a memory trail
leaning north-east. White layers of charcoal,
body bulk abated in fire and rain. Is this a porthole
between compartments? Repeopled as the trade route
now with noise of a car, this rondel points toward
an array of uprights and flankers, cup and ring marks
recording things unknown. Orbital grammar
might tell the stage of the year, or cry an ancient chad
was here. Master-cut, long-weathered forms
humble our mathematic reach. Wet hatches you can't skip
yield wholeness, half in wreckage from Ardrishaig
to Loch Awe, a winding film of those adrift and home.

Botanic Kingdom

Now will I the werd rehers
Wyntoun, *Oryginale Cronykil of Scotland*

You have to make it funny

a full moon

must be one
of their spotlights

Disco shafting in emerald shift
she has him
snort a line from her thigh

while stilted witches step twelve foot high
from the Devil's lap

he's a gangster with a dagger
thinking no man real
will snuff the hero

but a piper leads through black pines
to show the other Mac

Balscaddan Cottage

only in his dreams is a man really himself
John Butler Yeats

You take the glass from your bedroom window
so sea-spray soaks the bed—
a fishing smack gone out from harbour.
You sleep among rhododendrons and rocks
so you forget a morning lesson.
You climb the hill and see her in a dog-cart,
red hair gusting over belladonna eyes.
There is no knowing what I might do, she says,
I have such plots of war and peace.
She builds herself into the story, a witch
who plays with Time as gulls swoop
at the blue door of a white house. All voices
she has, pushing a man to texture breath
beyond metallic, a trick on board that's later true.

Blanchland

Hollow beneath rugged moor, lingering chant
of monks in the wind. Life absorbed
within life, a sheep-fleece for limbs
stiff and sore. Cry of filmy spirit, streaked
in a downward arc to forage. Makes earthswing
in a wink, this messenger by peck and probe
would carve stories—*coor-lee*—over silence.
Other faced but kin we follow the peat-stained burn
dropping from an engine house shell.
Was, is—as the V of scribble before mullioned window
a portrait of escape. She has the key to her bosom
riding squelchy fells. Guested in the north tower
by birch-log blaze we rehabit a beating heart
through unstrict hours, talk poets back to the table.

Whitby - 1

Mares'-tails high in the sky
then a faint hollow boom
over glass. A stranger
on the companion-way
steps behind
the skeleton nave, King Laugh
lifting a through-stone

A ship, she doesn't mind
the hand on the wheel, sweeps
in froth between granite piers
to pitch on sand

Must keep writing, big and little
for strength to combat
the nip, the feast at beauty's throat

Whitby - 2

Watchtower over wave-road

a camp

with tablet navigation

closely wired

the eye catches (you should go

to Scarborough)

Someone in black folds

with hands clasped

looks up at the rose

kin

of a serpent-stone or jet heart

pulled from a chink

Window veins

backlit hold a moor-strider's cry

Grosmont

for Patrick Lee

Chug and puff and cheep, we come to an abbey
that's vanished, though there are spoil tips
in Crag Cliff wood and the slopes are seamed
with iron
                    here's a coaling tower
beside the Deviation Shed and a table to turn
engines round

                              the tunnel mouth has battlements
as if an outlaw were to walk through
by a greasy rail

                              well it is a channel smashed
to Beckhole, casting off ropes and pulleys
so wagons will draw

pip peep with steam, 1-in-49 will just let us climb

Renishaw

Yesterday stretches, clinker black—blind eye holes
under fortress teeth
                                                        trees stark
                                    against lion
                        furnace glare

Statues from lake and wood
                        bid you

                                to southern sky
                                            in northern walls

                                creaking stairs, corridor-miles
                        past an elephant with slaves

ostrich feathers at the head of the bed

                        a drowned boy's kisses
as river weed   bring red-green dreams to print

Peterborough Chronicle

The abbot disturbed at his meal
cursed the house and left to dispense law
at Castor, and a servant failing to light
a fire cried likewise the Devil take it
whereupon flames rose to the roof
till bells broke and on the ninth day
the wind sent burning splinters to his abode.

———

A new abbot. It was Sunday. They heard
blowing and crying, and in the night
came hunters on black horses and goats
with wide eyes, and hounds barking
through Lent. And they called him forth
and sent him to Cluny where he yet
swore to return but was by stone prevented.

Osney Abbey

Nothing, only shadows, but Aubrey
had three faces drawn and got
the manner of building. A tower and vaults
to counter magpie chatter or quiet souls
in purgatory, with grain then wool accounts
to balance and make envy. You can see
pinnacles over Frog island where
the raised railway shakes, and feel the smart
of scalding liquor. An abbot like a bell
encompassed by water begs to go elsewhere
but wouldn't lose his fish-pond. Hobbes
who doesn't much care for logic
traps jackdaws with cheese on a string
but the owner of this arch says the site is safe.

Botanic Garden, Oxford

The king moved forth and broken

Danby, founder of physic   a year gone

leads whether by design   to a yew planted

shooting with child branches

that are dry and straggly

hung from wizened bark

A lute over centuries
may resound

as a mandrake (come back in winter)
lies dormant in deep soil
ready to bleed   and shriek

the pitcher plant will gobble an intruder
who tumbles and drowns

these several gums of war stock Paradise

Great Tew - 1

A crack in the sky, a streak of silver
hangs over talk
in a walled garden

here books can breathe, or did
on a summer evening

everything to question
but not to wreck

        as the lime trees
        argue

under wingtip or sword

        one in despair
        will thrust
        through a gap

the bluebells levelling would fill

Great Tew - 2

To climb deeper
into this seat

a leaf of rebellion
pokes

daring the spiral

to floors uncertain, door unhinged—

a plaster face without mouth or chin

dolls the ledge

has you scan

a letter from Lincoln's Inn

declining favour

for marble beneath a chandelier

gets faction-struck
and no grace abounds

Ditchley

for Robert Sheppard, returning a dedication

Where d'you get wit when the clamp is on
with platforms denied at the drop
of a bleeding head? True, you can straddle
causes: one afraid of peace couldn't hope
to keep his state. But where's the space
to turn a cup now tables are set
for straighter business. Grymes the giant
laid a ditch oblique which this timber hall follows
with stag-horns mounted. Eliza put her foot
on the map, straining, and a poet will be civil
till a dial fucks time. If the present moment's
all our lot and truth's in the second bottle
those early marks leave us rambling
down tracks modal only to do otherwise.

Rollright Stones

How stories arrive, a track along the ridge
between counties where two streams
drop. Here's the King-pointer, his army of rotten teeth
and huddled conspirators. Railings and lichen
half-hide the slabs uncountable.

Crane your ear to know but maybe it's just
the wind whispers. A village below
can't be seen when a mound lies between—
so the player loses, flesh turning to rock.

People cut chips for luck or move a block
to make a bridge and the hugging arrangement
won't be undone. You can dig but you'll find nothing,
neither a Dane vader or sacrifice. Bits of
an early world hold more without the rummage.

Devil's Quoits

Ghost of an airfield   is it   under alehoof
        to see (inside out)   a gravel moonscape
                bombers   flare-lit
                      vault   to hammer Scharnhorst

                                                the devil
                                          interrupted
                                    on Beacon Hill

                tosses
            his playthings
              to encircle
                a field

great coagulates   put back
by aerial pinpoint
what if the centre's scooped awry

Prior Park

Out of the yowl of Lilliput Alley and frowzy steam,
a showpiece for stone that's easy to cut. Honey-block retreat
high over valley and bowl, a sweep of exact vision
at a looser pitch. Allworthy? With an actor's bite
through stepped wilderness.

Ghost horns of deer
give you the enclosed picture, a runic triangle
for a lord and a black brachet. To seek and find
by sound or scent a velvet beast in a strange country.
All manner gentle by scutched grovework
as a spring line descends.

Rescue-ground
with grotto, lake and graffitied bridge
lets in other feet. A small west gate newly plotted
opens a trail to the skyline, so dignity breathes
with rougher twists—re-earthing our way-post home.

Lansdown Tower

What are forms? The heart is everything
when you run up a shaft
to know the stars and look over the land below
forgetting crashes of a caliph's dream.
A belvedere is not enough, go higher
to mark the top of a green slope
and live out a singular bent
with paper pure as the day it was printed.
Take the spirit in stages, from crimson silk
and Etruscan vases, up a spiral of carpet and iron
to the gilded lantern, giddy in a promise
to open downs and river, a world outcast
by normal pace. To spend poetically in the face
of badness, that's the lasting rhythmic break.

Nether Stowey

A spot to dig and think by sloping combes
and springy heath, watchful of water dripping
from a wheel and the stream that winds
through fern—a folio mind engaged with a fellow
or sloe in blossom, planning to be different
from what's laid out and faithful still
to a thrush's song, wool on the fence, a mirror
of a child's babble silver behind clouds

Tartarian tan-pits, a cottage with damp parlours
squeezed to the road, talk closed
where you lie sidelong, allegiance questioned
in fancy-points and fringes

yet he walks his garden strip to the bookroom
and climbs a mount to see (so jogs the day)

Ashley Combe - 1

Where servers come invisible, out of tunnels
beneath beeches and pine—a sea echo
in turrets, terraces. Her steps are ivy-wrapped,
the windows flake. Italy's a clock tower
with an empty circle. Can it go back, can it do
more than the figures put in? Her *tic*
(if thought is a theorem) goes through a guitar
to find they will, punch slots
black as a weaver's print to turn a bet right:
or if a horse stumbles along the track
something is learnt, maybe the break built in.
A wheel of number this enchantress
draws in a vault, blue-eyed by a father's stain
so the shift will read off hidden letters.

Ashley Combe - 2

Pheasants behind wire, laurel, rhododendron—
        a crumbling maze, forbidden. Never
take a proof untried when the thing itself is there
        with botheration. You mark a ledge,
a set of tiers, and what's performed will splay
        into new sense. The prepared key
fixes and spills: spine crawling through stricture,
        feel-notches of escape.

A name short, ancient, vocalic
        saves time to spell on the strand
below: 'A' scored twice with a 'D' between,
        Lace (less) love, angling from birth
to find a core that drives. Think a bath house
        in rock, waves before fire.

Ludlow Castle

Normans made me   a limestone chunk
on a hill   where rivers meet
to watch over   woods, pasture
the base   in a line
pitched against   an older claim
with water bore   and food-pile
that make safe   the Marches
for they that obey   by rigged esteem

Brothers in a cycle   fight brothers
with grappling iron   and cannon
a Lady threatened   comes through the wild
a pointed window   nudging the dais
holds an echo   of struck out notes
now keep me solar   through darkest braid

Tretower

Light gleams at the end of a passage—spirit
from a cloven family who didn't inherit.
White plaster over woven branches,
a weather-stained octavo, is that a hand
pointing to the magic in slightest things?
Feel by stone and wood, steps imagined
to the garden with tang of herbs
and over the field a stream he'd wish to be
pulsing by tree roots. What use this cylinder
nine foot-thick in a ragged curtain
as pikes and horses clash on a distant hill.
Back along the gallery a love-twist
holds up a falling self and empty inside
the hall sings between wind-braces.

Blickling Hall

Arms thrust forward, yew then brick
to embrace who comes. Head and shoulders
elegantly reared over a heart that's hidden.
Pencilled flesh, still young, eyes green
to beckon in stages—just a flush of daring
in a set of manners. Serried here is the reach
that went with a banquet, pad upon nail.

A gamester who loses a ruby brooch
will gallop to find her mate, hold a pistol
at the coach, speak low-pitched and take the booty.
And so breeds a habit, roistering for another
chest of bullion, though a highway captain
won't kill. Her beauty mark shines by the moon
but nothing can avert what's built to undo.

Felbrigg

In by the Lion's Mouth forked beeches
stopping a northerly

bark smooth as skin
before cordage

backway steps

to stone, flint, brick patched Jacobean
at second reach

faces in a tier
of mullion-light

one in the great breach will have no truck
with Ship Money

another fly buzzing paws his books

while he who'd kiss a horse-breaker
(term exploded) punches your ticket

Shardeloes

Grass, horse chestnut, drive—a green domain in hills
that stretch forever

it's framed in the window
as she looks out
striking the pane with a riding crop

raised by the wind and sun
she would have it
a golden slope
with earrings, ruby dress and hat

the portraits stare down
as her bare calf pokes from a chair
by Adam's chimney-piece

she will have her broke lord, a gypsy clutched
at the river bottom (storm-start lashing a portico)

Horsley Towers

Suddenly, out of the shade of woods
and a stretch of fields—Italy or the Loire valley
in a spatchcock dream: a flint clock tower
with creamy cylinder turrets, a Rhenish steeple-tower
beyond, a cloister laid on drainpipe columns
with a tunnel beneath, a porthole floor
so the eye will drop. Ada welcomes a visitor
beneath her father in Albanian dress

We are only different in our differences
says the engine ordered to perform, eating
its own tail. A little more and the pitched sounds
will show on screen, all the steps through
in whatever scene—a horse clearing
that will print out her looped selves tomorrow

Ham House - 1

Scratches her finger on the wall
by the fireplace

a jib door
to a private closet

Medea one breast bare

a serpent bird coaxes
with vulture beak
and crimson feathers

Bess who made the place

plots with her tail so the Duke takes
as his

what others did behind his back

a clipped geometric *I know what it's like*

echoes feral in empty ice drum

Ham House - 2

Back from the river   by oaks and crows
in surprise

an avenue of limes

god with an upturned urn

ghost of a canal   to the water gate

as the eye turns   from brick

to Cherry Garden   and Wilderness

reason

the draughtsman disturbs

hornbeam tunnels   iron railings

Melancholy Walk   hill beyond

green on green   a Cabal

never met in stone

moves

Eltham Palace

Art silk will get you a hall with a hammer-beam roof
and a red rose grafted on a white. Why not add
a minstrels' gallery to echo the film version?
A glazed dome meets old timber gables
as a lady tilts her foot, snake tattoo above the ankle—
what would survive without an update?
A Roman soldier and a Viking stand before
views of Italy but everything's the latest:
a magicoal fire with Tudor braziers, music piped
by hidden speakers, a booth with a coinbox-phone.
All dust sucked through hoses to a cylinder
in the basement. Jongy the lemur might bite you
but he's happy in a bamboo forest with a ladder
to help him to bed. Deco's a test of intention.

Temple of Mithras, Walbrook

To bring back light: step down
into murk, walk on stone
in a marshy course. Coin with soft possibility
keeps the rite alive (fellows' secrets
behind a curtain). A mark or a small scar
on the forehead is the bull's flank
asking for release. This pit will run blood
from star to star. You're a raven
then a lion and finally a father
in seven stages. Out of mouldering
beeswax on wood the script addresses
'Mogontius'. A straddle of stream and street,
the cellar is a rotten sun that can rise
to profit whoever comes.

Grenfell Tower

The adjectives can wait
when control slips: who
in the grid   (who isn't
escaped, who in remove
chose   the proofing and
panels, who   laid shield
to shield   with airways,
who didn't box pipes or
link an alarm,   who said
stay put   in a pack that
shouldn't give.   Empty
eyes stare out of a black
frame just north of easy
terraces——stucco clad.

More London

They're bricking up the rill
so zombies won't trip

chevron ripples
in a limestone channel

the guide-ribbon
on a course
between battleship plates

you can pass if you don't take a picture
sharply observed from glass edges

sovereign wealth
has you move on grey slate
by grey metal

I thought they were kissing but she was
just reading his smartphone

Abbey Road

Land shaft north   talkback voices
from mono to infinity
painters & models, a batsman still at the crease

up steps through a grey door to varnished wood
four and a half miles of cable   girls everywhere
like ants in a cupboard

a minute out of one tape   half-minute out of another
cut into pieces   flung in the air   a carousel

the orchestra's in the canteen   waiting

a loop slowed with a pencil
faders right down at point of impact
then right up

breath in echo plates
a heartbeat on the floor

Oak Hill

for Lesley Higgins

First child on first height, breezy air over haze
in treadset surround, here with marigold breath
by the sliced core of a haystack your arm can fancy
touching the sky—he would climb fearless
an elm in the garden and walk barefoot
the long grass to a pool or another ridge, joyed
wild where brambles make a sort of mail
like Knight's graving. Of all marks it is the cared-for
crown of trees that shapes this sense, spoke-wise
clubs of green and scanty leaf-stars, a star-knot
worked round to give ear reach. Dappled outline
under curd-barrow clouds, a map to figure
a way back which goes on: relation loosing
the heart that lies   a spicule blot in an inkstand

St Anne, Limehouse

i.m. Derrick Woolf

You don't need a crypt below when it can rise
in stages, white before your bobbing shade

seventeen steps to a door
between massive columns

a dome then a tower
and another
to the lantern

as to think a way through
yesterday's mist

where a yellow claw might beckon
from its mossy pyramid

empty chambers loom, impossible to reach
an oval to stave off foul spirits
floating weightless in a stretched square

Petworth

A parcel of dells and hills from which you can see
for miles

the stone wall just a division

Stane Street over the down

Blake's cottage

that won't measure

the flight of thought

as a star enters his left foot

a world remade   with copper, acid

against the trooper's blast   under hireling terms

hard to bend wrath

into care   lark song   why would you leave

park and border   writing wild thyme

calls back   surely   one last judgment

Place House (Titchfield Abbey)

All the church must downe with the steple … for plukyng downe of the church is but a small matter myndyng (as we doubt not but you woll) to buyld a Chaple

John Crayford & Roland Lathom, King's Commissioners, to Thomas Wriothesley, 2 Jan. 1537

A cluster of starlings high in an oak tree
beyond the outer wall—black specks
on a green curl of chatter. One elite thrust up
replaces another, propped or housed
with riches. An embattled gatehouse tower
rears through the nave, roofless
while a window marks the playhouse room.
Under gaping chimney-mouths we walk
the plan, cloister-court to great hall
in a pullback to base: tiles that show St John's
arms with monkey supports or a fleur-de-lys
between facing birds. Scenes performed
lie quiet, filtered by rain and sunlight.
No lord no monk encaustic presses this form.

Meon Shore

i.m. Angela Selerie Meech

The tide rolls out and the sinking sun
casts a streak over sea and shore

a yellow-orange shimmer
over low water

forcing between dark weed to sand ripples
laid in a sworl

black-headed gulls cluster as specks
trampling back

you are a child eating grains in a garden pit
you are a sailor leaning with the wind
you are a painter finding the signal tint

somewhere in this gold reach
the heart you had for all
keeps an airy cell that no current can forget

Out of an English Pole

for Robert Hampson

2017

I

You never know what may be of use, as a place
carefully looked at once. Smell of earth, damp foliage,
hollow beneath the roots of a large tree. It seems
the cord of silence can never snap. Silver fastens
upon a man's mind, a blotch across windows
full of stars. Worse than thirst at sea or hunger
where others are fed. To scramble back to the spot
with teeth that rattle, a vague form
erect in the shadow. It hasn't meant anything,
there are no words for what you'd want
to say, but it rings deep, a throb of drums
you must face or shirk. Beyond blinking humbug
to force action when squirts get empty
the best thing, as a sanitized plate, is to tell the tale.

II

All is light, light, and the boat seems to be falling
through it, that glitter of a vast surface
where even the beginning is all illusion. It's the East
speaking in a Western voice. I suppose a man
with a secret locked in his breast
loses buoyancy—it lies heavy like a Jubilee coin
in a leather box. Behind any white drill-suit
there are years compressed, stuff to ruminate
stepping from the cabin. Who's that
fugitive in wreaths of steam, screed on a rose panel
dared into conception? It leaves
a saving mark in waves to help out the mess
of strangeness. If there were only a word to stand
at the back of all words, landfall would be less a strain.

III

Haven't had time to be dull for the last

I don't know

how many

years

now the piece has to be played to another tune
and in much slower time

scraps of old adventure

sparks struck   with a pinch of romance

in the commercial kitchen

or whiffs of scent   from a walled garden

moozik

tinkling

a prosperous passage

core phrases to enchant

IV

A find made in a box of books

in a street that no longer exists

just a medallion

in the drabs of the pavement

stirs a binnacle light, brazen

to ride

the spring-flood   of memory

spunyarn rovings

over a glass

homelike at the jetty   in dissolving contact

no chance-comer now

from too much dice

but festal in confab   topic on topic

best rig texted   through mere rag

Tuning Tomorrow

2018-2019

Triologue

for Alan Halsey at 70

How random is random? Stein dined with Housman
and they talked of fish. Her voice sounds like three panes
of cracked glass but beer can bubble up a stanza.
Are you a hill-man or a library man with eye decumbent
(there's no word now for 'flyttand'). Well here's a jug
and a leather bag, you don't need a deer hunt
to eager the blood. Read *her* with *her* for less, a leap
beat to a holy gauge. It's not the thing said but the way
of saying, we don't need to know that the palace door
is Roderick Usher's mouth. Lingo, lingo that's the pencil
which draws, as this lifting belly isn't a sleeper
with a yen for lard. Will willows bear pears and girls
go in gold? The stems are there—if we don't
viral them out. It's a long story and impossible to tell.

Questions Present

i.m. John James

You could hear it a tiny island in thirty nine
or now as she sags downstream
a brigand at the castle talks clubland electric
like some trick of sun in valley mist

a cool fetch ordinary enough to pass
hums a phrase that is half the meadow in a poster
putting the fruits of fooling, fuzz and lilt
with a gable lozenge and diamonds in the first storey

it's us in purple armour, is it
to gliss a gap between heritage lines

if one's no longer here his belt in the yard
has a smudge of boot polish to keep the rap
unblazoned—taking care of no business
makes the shine go true

Crack in Space

We were holding a house-warming party in a place
with a passage that ran the length of the ground floor
but no one had come. Food and wine were piled
on the stairs and I fell over a crate, knocking my head
in the dark. Something seemed to stroke my skull
and the sutures parted, letting another self rise
into the air. I was in a corridor whose walls
were dripping with molten pitch, and a woman
dressed in a white shift wound some thread
round my thumb, leading me past hooks that tried
to enclose and trap. I found I was in a wardrobe
when suddenly hordes of people broke through—
our absent guests. Accosted, one said 'Don't you
know, there's a sacred site up on the hillside beyond.'

Jongleur

I walk into a strange country where froth
emerges from the ground as if the sea has bored
a channel to bring stuff back. A hoarding says
a roast goose will fly to your table and music will play
without touching a button. Somewhere west
but really here there's an immense club
where anybody can go for broke and one fast car
will collect your winnings, shouldered safely in bed

The house rises a hundred floors above and drops
a hundred floors below, with silver sockets
that might yield a view but won't roll or pop—
it's a dizzy world that's frozen, a pound and shudder
crying *jock-a-mo chock-a-mo* in dry blue ink
when me is reserved for what they in cabal believe

Batable Land

We are now ever two bodies
trying to leave or stay

while ice a ghostly rubric
breaks at the pole

Gog and Magog say they're elect
like travels of the glass

no but no but no but
singles an issue to beat the way

bullets
twisting in air

think you'll rid, think you'll embrace
face-connected in a field

but who'd stand up to lie level
only will-o'-the-wisp

Liquin Base

A stream trickles under the dining-room floor
and the boards seem to quake

        what do you think, I'll ask my puppet
        a subject seen through a glass of ale

you can't hear its face
only needed in nodding

                all ours the blissblade
                bringback
                stanza to stick

        red on blue on white
        me and my kite are all right

if it glosses you must not think
it'll prove a fix, this rumble skipscape
hides the spectre   deals beyond the finish

Mock Saviour

Keep your friends close by
but keep your enemies even closer

(old proverb)

A dream of getting an empire back
with bootstrap fastness   a stamp of self
to kick those bodies just held together by glue

what's done in me another does

he's a wall-eyed hero shorter than you think
who passes unscathed with a flaming torch
through the cedar-wood

oh, it's a rich romance to read and reckon true
if dread construes the residue

he'd like to live on like a phoenix-tree
becoming one in the daily duel

self-fond, self-furious   he'll switch values
to gild an idol thigh and throat
then crash to the ground reduced to powder

Spillway

Only much furrowed, eight foot from trough
to crest, no no in the second dogwatch
the bulkhead's broken into shards and slivers
and a thunder of foam's in the glory hole

down between the storm's knees
who remains to navigate,
there are fingers kinked and gnarled like trees
lapping slime at the cabin door

whose are these dead white eyes
upturned from a dark brown floor, weed tuft
brows wanting the upper berth to drop

your wheel's jammed, no there's none
to hold with a dree moan
in this box that presses through blank space

Growth Hack

All we can do is sort our house out
but the failure failure april first
to find even p.s. we love you cursed
agreement for any so-spout

lution offers no hope that there's shout
any way p.s. we love you versed
out of this with options april burst
it's nailed-on mad to feel canny about

we know what you don't want, idol-struck
but we still don't know what you want
the sphinx is an open book to your ruck

p.s. we love you except for Lamont
but let's not boil the ocean for a fuck
just coax your creature to speak in a font

Overbridges and Underbridges

Get your message at our store know what's cool
the tallgo tellgo tillgo tollgo has an opal window
that charges any screen-face with marsh light
will work 24s a winking wire thrust from stoveblack
stuff you needn't start an account it'll roll out
soon with more at the core like d'you wan a drink
could be d'you wan a drain but in all removes
keep the scrilla from a paigon whatever the plug

If blizzard decides to buff the F out of azerite traits
you'll have to retrieve your gear to make sure
it isn't better now or you'll have a box of laughing
bricks zinnia-red that won't amp the head
for municasion, splain it you can't flag by word
ema lema looks draipsin to a fed but not to a bruv

Ambage

after Julio Cortázar

I they see the moon rose, we hurt me
at the eyes behind, you the blonde woman
was the clouds that race before my your
their faces. It's a meadow slope
and they were a couple, sparrows fluttering
in the shrubs. She wears a black fur coat
and touches his cheekbones gently
as the branches sway. He put his arm
around her waist, they kiss and he starts
to undress her. It is happening ten feet away,
I think I know how to look, they are tacked
with pins on the wall. She turns, a weathercock
deciding or decided, now the sun came
twice as strong, one laugh is a whip of feathers

Deep-speare Cuts the Mustard

If this sweet violet is your breath and cheek
forward in a hedge-bank or wood
it asks my pen in black lines to draw
what I would seek that others slam
sly from a hood whose craw won't venture
when your white-purple is nothing gross—
just rises from a creeping stem
as the vein indenture to stain a handler
minute by year in a willing dose.
'Our' for 'one' isn't shame or despair
its robed scent sings on ... way past prime
while a scrambler ate up with care
pushes his juddering jamb into chime.
Given a cup for features hot to steal
we'll play ourselves out in a sharper tweak

Neural Base

If all the sounds that fit are put through a tube
to get the feel of a thinking frame
and every idea's embedded to the last cube
like angels in armour riding a flame

if all characters pass through a filter gate
from the vast reach of language space
where add and shuffle use their wanted weight
with grace to chase the most singular place

if these can make a poem's parts complete
in cram crawl code that lays a thread
winding digits to the hard conceit

still there will hover in a restless head
one secret, one wonder at least
which cannot by any orifex be released

Counterstory

Who touched who
                    squeezed a shoulder
                       smelt hair
                          licked an ear
                             held for a beat too long

             not to be a machine

      you see, don't you
      no, don't *you* see

the personal vibe   a soft hole in the middle

                    he brushes her arm as she reaches
                    for the mic

             [wind back] she pulls it from him

      ambit gambit rambit
outrage is a helluva drug

Open Juncture

There	bluebirds	perching	on freight	trains
here	painted	actors	rolling	through
when	yellow	artfully	streaked	quatrains
always	deliver	on cue	what's	true
now	questions	emerge	that	throb
still	constrained	with	force	inside
as	curving	sense	deflects	a sob
before	conceits	to move	the cloud	applied
again	ahead	a dark	surround	blear-shut
for	silverer	chance	giddily	on track
ever	springs	in tune	lying	well cut
so	at edge	of heart	to breathe	in slack
yet	all rung	farther	by fall	and swell
among	random	courses	this ghost	can gel

Flower Piece

after Gerhard Rühm

the tulip craps on the lawn
the violet farts in the gardener's hand
the forget-me-not spews into tissue paper
the carnation spits on its stem
the orchid jerks off in the girl's fingers
spattering her sleeve
the rose stinks of sweat and menstrual blood
the may bell drops snot on the tablecloth
the lily pisses in the vase
the hyacinth belches

stem and stalk
go death still
don't try
to talk back

Stone Record

The mill wheel clicks as it turns, a sparkle in gloom
of sheep-silver   *for profit*   *for profit*   on the gush
and   *no pro ... fit*   *no ... oo ... prof ... it*
when the water's cut and the great disc slows

its groan has the print of walking in a circle
with patches of thyme and hare-bells
or again as felt between your shoulder blades
it must be the aisle of some walled-in place

a cry and a luminous streak, a knife sawing
through tissue, you think to gauge with the latest tech
she's there and she's not in the long dry grass
or green-tinted against black-hewn steps

a hold-over next to the ground   you fall across
only one in the sensitive now   can see

Ditch Scan

The sniff of sap-wet stalks

shine of an old pebble
by yellow-capped fungus

spear-sharp leaves against

high hung blue

a clinging spume
or tiny splash

that's us dug into stirring

weed pungent

by hum in hollow

root-got promise to be

wood water rock

name-joins
in strife of spirit

Albion Edge

each thing his turne do's hold
Herrick

A calf becomes a young knobber or brocket,
later a spire or pricket, then a staggart
and finally a hart

quits a tangled covert to seek the open moor

as a broken limb of an ash tree
stretches its fingers
signing the way

he's a ten-point king, the self we'd wish
seen in snatches

not to be hollow-proud
and gobble the understorey

but equal footed to run and track
in unclosed grass and fern the hunter's
a camera can leap the broil or level

Devil's Wood

Tell me why you're the whip handle
of a hearse driver
or the cross to hang
a hero or thief

easy found
furrowed in chalk

a kind of poet
with cream-green circlets

spicy-sweet and sad

•

When cut I bleed
thick wine

cry as a pipe
ring as a harp

lend parts for any ill in stanza-store

The Return

It's a habit this beastly reading; this gorge and glint and fever
all at second-hand . . . But once you're in, there's no recovery
—Walter de la Mare

A gliding mist
in narrow quarters

a stone cracked
head to foot

blunt, green
encircled with thorns

I should like a peep
who wouldn't

the Hand has lost
its 'n' and 'd'

would that be Stranger
its 'g' a twisted tail

why should we be else
the face taken

Debordering

for Henry Woudhuysen

It isn't ordered, the lines laid out in a furrow
and signatures threaded, with heed to what will go
down a coastal edge or hilly bend, parts
muddied and crumpled. It is frayed and foxed
like lost remembrance and a page here and there
is torn, someone's cut the top margins too close
and a reader has scribbled sharply in the void
with a long cursive 'a' beside lozenge marks

whose text, whose territory is this, where a board
is filled with a waste leaf and first thoughts
branch into other folds. An eye will roll
that hears over heard in inky travels, thumbing
it doesn't happen or it's not valid
to a green passage through blistered wilderness

Traces

after Bernard Noël

These lines inked on pebble-skin, a plan
for a creature with moon eyes
shut within brick
throw themselves back to our gaze

the thing goes misty in thought
as scaffolding in air

jointed bones take flight
ranging beyond what's given

you it he's a suspended state
deedal and barely mooted

a wall of nothing
where words persist
then sink
in briny vision

Night-stepper

At the end of a white trail
in nowhere hours
the maker thinks he's rocked
the level line, steeping a beat
to let all the voices
ring their stuff, fa-la, la-la
in bladderwrack and surf
traced on a desk apart.

An engine-house
feels out beneath—chip chip
for a lode—as rods, chains
grind and swing
even in granite silence
the gulls and wind reverse.

Acknowledgments

Thanks are due to the editors and publishers who first issued some of the texts included here. A particular debt is owed to Paul Green for publishing the sequence *Elizabethan Overhang* (Spectacular Diseases, 1989). Other books from which material has been taken include:

Azimuth (Binnacle Press, 1984)
Puzzle Canon (Spectacular Diseases, 1986)
Tilting Square (Binnacle Press, 1992)
Danse Macabre (Ispress & West House Books, 1997)
Le Fanu's Ghost (Five Seasons Press, 2006)
Music's Duel (Shearsman Books, 2009)
Hariot Double (Five Seasons Press, 2016)
For Robert: An Anthology (Poetics Research Centre, Royal Holloway & the Institute of the Electric Crinolines, 2017)

Outtakes from *Days of '49* reflect discussion with Alan Halsey concerning themes and strategies realized in the book itself. Thanks also to him for scans of images for the current book.

Various poems from 1997 onwards draw on expeditions made with Frances Presley, whose alertness to the natural world is always a source of inspiration.

Notes: part or main context

29 'Rude Stone': Rudston monolith.

50 'Tundale': cf. the *Vision of Tundale*, which may have influenced Bosch's *Garden of Earthly Delights* (Museo del Prado, Madrid).

60 '29': additional poem outside the 28-sonnet sequence, handwritten into the signed limited edition of *Elizabethan Overhang*.

63-89 The section graphics for *Tilting Square* are by Gavin Selerie, with numerals by Julie Arnall. Selerie discusses the structural significance of these images in *Into the Labyrinth* (Argotist ebooks).

68 'Metabasis': written soon after the dismantling of the Berlin wall; 'Bronze'—the statue of Victory over the Brandenburg gate.

92 'Utility': cf. the non-conventional sense implied by Shelley in his comment, 'Whatever strengthens and purifies the affections, enlarges the imagination . . . is useful' (*A Defence of Poetry*).

93 'Transport and Misnaming': Puttenham's terms for metaphor and metonymy from *The Arte of English Poesie*.

93 'Aspic': written after a Nile expedition in Egypt.

97 'Dante to Cino of Pistoia': line 2 is diverted from its literal sense, which refers to Dante's ninth year, the time when he first saw Beatrice at the May Feast.

127 'Capricho Oscuro': Cervantes's landing at Denia and subsequent stay in Valencia, October 1580; a double sonnet.

130 'Saint Variations': Gertrude Stein, *Four Saints in Three Acts* (1927) and *Picasso* (1938).

131 'Leapfrog': Goya, *Boys Playing Leapfrog* (Museo de Bellas Artes, Valencia).

147 'Limbo Line': *Death Line* (Sherman); the British Museum.

157 'Quartet': Beethoven, op. 132.

163 'Thriller': *The Tango Lesson* (Sally Potter).

165 'Prado Gaze': Titian, *Venus and the Organ Player* (Museo del Prado, Madrid).

166 'The Clowns': José Gutiérrez Solana, *Payasos* (Museo Nacional Centro de Arte Reina Sofía, Madrid).

166 'Stop the Beginning': Matthew Lewis, *The Monk*; Buñuel and Carrière, *Le Moine* (screenplay, 1971). Title: Ovid, *Remedia Amoris*, 91, tr. 'F.L.' (1600).

168 'View and Plan': El Greco, *View and Plan of Toledo* (Museo del Greco, Toledo).

169 'Floating Nous': Cervantes, *Don Quixote*, II, 1 (Toledo setting).

171 'Posada': The Posada de la Sangre, frequented by Buñuel and fellow members of the 'Order of Toledo'; formerly thought to have been the site where Cervantes wrote some of his *Exemplary Novels*; destroyed during Franco's capture of Toledo, 1936.

172 'Exemplary Tales': 'The Glass Graduate' and 'The Force of Blood' in Cervantes, *Exemplary Novels*.

174 'The Weight': *Tristana* (Buñuel).

175 'Archpirate': Eustace the Monk, who spent a winter and summer with the devil, in an abyss beneath Toledo. See *Roman d'Eustache le Moine*.

178 'Folio Version': Jan Potocki, *The Manuscript Found in Saragossa*; *The Saragossa Manuscript* (Wojciech Has).

184 'Seed': cf. Nerval, 'à J[enn]y Colonna' (early version of 'Delfica'), which references Goethe, 'Kennst du das Land…', a poem some associate with the Persephone myth.

195–8 '*Danse Macabre* (Recension)': a reworking of Selerie's longer contribution to *Danse Macabre: Death & the Printers* (1997), with the context narrowed to Valencia, where, in 1474, the first Spanish printed book may have been produced. Although these sonnets have a more literal place within the *Twisted Circle* sequence, they seem to stand better apart. The 1997 book was a collaborative response to the earliest known illustration of a printing press, in a *Danse Macabre* sequence printed by Matthias Hus (1499).

204 'Imitation of Life': W. Grey Walter created two of the first electronic autonomous robots, Elmer and Elsie, in Bristol (1948–49; first press report, November 1949). Due to their shape and slowness of movement, they were described as tortoises.

205 'Tutor's Tale': Michael Innes, *The Journeying Boy* (1949)—perhaps the first nuclear-age detective story.

209 'Judgment': Marghanita Laski, *Little Boy Lost* (1949).

210 'Four Star Puzzle': *Follow Me Quietly* (1949), scripted by Anthony Mann and Lillie Hayward; alternate version of poem in *Music's Duel*.

212 'MoMA's Façade': first complete American performance of *Façade*, Museum of Modern Art, New York, 19 January 1949, given by Edith Sitwell and a six-piece orchestra (CD, 1994); her voice and the music were amplified through a screen that featured designs by Esteban Frances. Sitwell's selected poems, *The Canticle of the Rose*, was also published that year.

213 'Phantom Mannequin': Sheila Legge, the Surrealist Phantom in the 1936 London exhibition, died in January 1949. Her text 'I Have Done My Best for You' appeared in *Contemporary Poetry and Prose* (December 1936).

214 'The Mantic Stain': Ithell Colquhoun, essay in *Enquiry* (October 1949); *Autumnal Equinox* (oil on canvas), reproduced in the *Daily Mirror*, front page, February 1949.

215 'Hold Shot': John Craxton, *Head of a Sleeping Fisherman* (1949).

217 'Wonder Notch': Georg Mayer-Marton, *Llanthony Valley* (1949); otherwise the Vale of Ewyas ('place of battle').

218 'Portreath': Peter Lanyon, oil on strawboard (1949) and preparatory constructions.

220 'Domain of Arnheim': Magritte, *The Domain of Arnheim* (oil on canvas, 1949); Poe's story, reprinted in *The Centenary Poe* (Bodley Head, 1949).

221 'Gaugeless': Samuel Beckett, *The Unnamable*; *Waiting for Godot*; *Three Dialogues*.

222 'Shadow Real': article by C.A. Lejeune, *Leader Magazine* (23 April 1949).

223 'Bed Fare': J.B. Priestley, *Delight* (1949).

224 'Man on the Eiffel Tower': 1949 film based on Simenon's *La Tête d'un homme*, featuring Charles Laughton as Maigret and Franchot Tone as his adversary.

225 'Time Unpast': Jean-Paul Sartre, tr. Lloyd Alexander, *The Diary of Antoine Roquentin* (1949).

227 'Poet's Dream': Geoffrey Grigson, 'Where Coleridge Dreamt his Kubla Khan' (*Country Life*, March 1949).

227 'Maid of the Mist': Exhibition of Air-Photographs of Archaeological Sites (Ashmolean Museum, Nov. 1948–Feb. 1949), featuring the work of Major G.W.G. Allen, a pioneer in the field. See also his book *Discovery from the Air*, published posthumously (1984).

228 'Other Tears': 'Otras ruinas' (1948–49) at one stage titled 'Londres', reflects Cernuda's experience in England 1939–47.

231 'Armchair Reading': *The Reformation of St Jules* by Algernon Blackwood (from the TV series *A Strange Experience*, 1949).

231 'Scanners Live in Vain': Cordwainer Smith, 'Scanners Live in Vain' (1945; pub. January 1950); Paul Linebarger, letter to his daughter Rosana, October 1943.

232 'Humdrum Master': Miles Burton, *Death Takes the Living* (1949).

233 'Situational': Josephine Tey, *Brat Farrar* (1949).

234 'Field for Shadows': Phyllis Paul, *Camilla* (1949).

235 'China Spells': Jung, Foreword to *The I Ching or Book of Changes* (1949); Robert Payne, *Mao Tse-Tung: Ruler of Red China* (advance copy inscribed to Charles and Connie Olson, November 1949).

241 'Liminal': based on spectral appearances at the Theatre Royal, Bath.

242 'Cenci Face': draws on passages which concern the alleged portrait of Beatrice Cenci by Guido in two of Eleanor Le Fanu's

novels, a motif which also appears in her father J.S. Le Fanu's work. The picture haunted Melville, among others (see *Pierre* and *Clarel*).

244 'Looker's Likeness': *Night of the Demon* (Tourneur); J.S. Le Fanu, 'The Haunted Baronet'. Outtake.

248–49 'Playing Policy Blues' and 'Snatch It Back Blues': written for an issue of the magazine *Purge*, dealing with the Blair government era; scheduled for late 2007, this never appeared.

256 'Beneath the Lid': Steve Lacy Quintet, *Estilhaços* ('shrapnel'), the first jazz record released in Portugal; from a concert at the Cinema Monumental, Lisbon, February 1972. This was a period when the authorities were still clamping down on supposedly decadent music.

257 'Dance of Paroxysms': *A Dança dos Paroxismos* (1929), inspired by Leconte de Lisle, 'Les Elfes'.

258 'Library': Maria Helena Vieira da Silva, *Bibliothèque* (oil on canvas, 1949).

261 'Occultation': *The Letters of a Portuguese Nun* (Marianna Alcoforado).

264 'Santa Clara Moment': Monastery of Santa Clara, Coimbra; St Elizabeth (Isabella) of Portugal.

265 'Saudade': Inês de Castro.

274 'Parish Without': Pinewood Sanatorium, Wokingham, an area lying on Bagshot sands; here in 1958 Joe Harriott seems to have begun forming his notion of free form jazz.

280 'Tune as Weather': Joe Harriott, St Ives 1970.

281 'Pallatyne Knot': in the voice of Thomas Harriot, attending the marriage celebrations of Princess Elizabeth and Frederick, Count Palatine, February 1613; the Earl of Northumberland was Harriot's patron.

282 'Abyss': outtake, based on Camões, *The Lusiads*, canto VI.

284 'Jest Site': Brainford (i.e. Brentford), adjacent to Syon, had a reputation for risqué entertainment and illicit liaison in the early modern era; 12-line sonnet.

284 'Blood Vine': outtake, based mainly on Gerard's *Herbal*.

285 'Nightspell': *Sir Bevis* in chapbook form, as typical of a child's reading c. 1570; here drawing on the romance *Bevis of [South]Hampton*.

289 'Sounding Cylinder': contraction of an *Azimuth* outtake, 'Almost Not an Interval', without any word-change, in the context of Kate McGarrigle's death.

303 'Botanic Kingdom': *Macbeth*, promenade production starring Dannii Minogue, Botanical Gardens, Edinburgh, August 1999; 'werd' in the epigraph = weird (fate, destiny).

304 'Balscaddan Cottage': in Howth, where W.B. Yeats lived from 1881–82. He fell in love with Laura Armstrong, who performed in a play he wrote for her, *Vivien and Time*. She was later the model for Margaret Leland in *John Sherman*. See these works and *Autobiographies*.

304 'Blanchland': in the part of the Lord Crewe Arms built onto the old abbey, my partner and I were assigned the room where W.H. Auden stayed over Easter 1930; see also Walter Besant, *Dorothy Forster* (1884).

309 'Peterborough Chronicle': accounts of the abbey in 1116 and 1127 from the Middle English Laud manuscript and that in Latin by Hugh Candidus.

312–13 'Great Tew': Lucius Cary, Lord Falkland, whose house provided a retreat for scholars and poets in the 1630s, was killed at the Battle of Newbury, 1643. Clarendon observes, 'he died as much of the time as the bullet'. The present house, uninhabited, is Georgian with Gothic and Tudor additions.

314 'Ditchley': Ditchley Park, the poet Rochester's childhood home. Built or enlarged by Sir Henry Lee, c. 1592, it stood where the Menagerie is now situated.

320 'Blickling Hall': Margaret Lockwood's mansion Maryiot Cells in *The Wicked Lady* (Arliss).

322 'Shardeloes': Deverill Court in *The Gypsy and the Gentleman* (Losey).

323 'Horsley Towers': home counties residence of Earl and Lady (Ada) Lovelace; exterior location for Taskerlands in *The Stone Tape* (1972) which features attempted data storage of sounds and images lingering within an ancient room.

324-25 'Ham House': Elizabeth Murray, Duchess of Lauderdale; Henry (or William G.) Ferguson, *Medea Casting Spells Among Ruined Sculpture*; 'Garden of Reason' exhibition (2012).

330 'Oak Hill': Gerard Manley Hopkins grew up in Oak Hill, Hampstead, 1852–63, returning during Oxford vacations and in subsequent years to visit his family. Much of the area was still rural; see Hopkins, diaries, journals and notebooks. He and his siblings pored over the pictures in Charles Knight's *Old England*.

332 'Petworth': 'William Blake in Sussex' exhibition, Petworth House (2018). Elizabeth Ilive, Countess of Egremont, commissioned several works from Blake, including *A Vision of the Last Judgment* (1808). He was based at Felpham from 1800 to 1803.

335–39 *Out of an English Pole*: words or phrases extracted from twenty or more works by Joseph Conrad; written, with progressive explosion of form, to mark a scholar's retirement.

352 'Deep-speare Cuts the Mustard': imagined computer-take on Shakespeare sonnet 99 in relation to the whole series.

362 'Traces': Noël's 60-line poem 'Les états de l'air' formed the preface to the catalogue of Vieira da Silva's exhibition, *Perspective labyrinthe, dessins* (Galerie Jeanne Bucher, Paris, 1982); one of the drawings is titled 'Dédale'.

www.ingramcontent.com/pod-product-compliance
Ingram Content Group UK Ltd.
Pitfield, Milton Keynes, MK11 3LW, UK
UKHW041949190726
13854UKWH00004B/1870

9 781848 616899